Our Planet at the Limit

How we overcome the growth paradigm
and become happier

Diplomatic Council Publishing

Helmut von Siedmogrodzki

Our Planet at the Limit

How we overcome the growth paradigm
and become happier

Diplomatic Council Publishing

1st edition 2025

All books published by Diplomatic Council Publishing are carefully compiled. Nevertheless, the authors, editors and publishers accept no liability whatsoever for the accuracy of the information, notes and advice contained herein or for any printing errors.

© 2025 Diplomatic Council (DC) Publishing, Mühlhohle 2, 65205 Wiesbaden, Germany
Email: info@diplomatic-council.org
Web: www.diplomatic-council.org

All rights reserved, in particular those of translation into other languages. No part of this book may be reproduced in any form - by photocopying, microfilming or any other process - or transferred or translated into a language that can be used by machines, in particular data processing machines, without the written authorisation of the publisher. The reproduction of product designations, trade names or other trademarks in this book does not justify the assumption that they may be freely used by anyone. Rather, they may be registered trademarks or other legally protected marks even if they are not specifically labelled as such.

All content in this book reflects the views and opinions of the author. These do not necessarily reflect the views and/or opinions of the Diplomatic Council and/or its members. The author is solely responsible for the texts, including all illustrations and graphics.

Note on gender-appropriate language

In this work, as in all books published by DC Publishing, the gender masculine, such as "scientist", "manager" or "expert", always refers to the gender-independent term, i.e. all (!) genders. All deviations from this rule are clearly labelled linguistically, for example with words such as "male" or "female".

For reasons of better readability, gender symbols or the designation "(m/f/d)" are completely omitted.

Scientific notation

In this book, the simpler spelling CO2 is always used instead of the correct scientific notation for chemical formulas such as CO_2, to increase readability.

Bibliographic information of the German National Library

The German National Library lists the publication in the German National Bibliography; detailed bibliographic data is available on the Internet at http://dnb.d-nb.de. Printed in the Federal Republic of Germany.

Printed: Libri Plureos GmbH, Friedensallee 273, 22763 Hamburg

Design, cover, typesetting: IMS International Media Services, Wiesbaden

Print ISBN: 978-3-98674-125-9
E-Book ISBN: 978-3-98674-126-6

For my sons Arndt und Michael

Contents

Foreword 9
Time for a paradigm shift 13
Limits to growth 17
    The Growth Mantra 18
    Society in transition 21
    Growth and socio-ecological balance..................................... 22
    The decade of action... 26
Living in abudance... 29
    The throwaway society.. 29
    Wrong incentives... 32
    Fight for the habitats.. 36
Growth on Credit 41
    The debt trap 43
    Too big to fail 48
    The dead end 51
    The flood of money... 54
Trust in Innovation 63
    Artificial Intelligence.. 64
    Limits of the progress 66
Capitalism versus Socialism.. 77
The future-proof company.. 83
    Agility and adaptability.. 84
    Sustainability is not a strategy.. 88
    Entrepreneurship as a service.. 95
    Globalization versus regionalization..................................... 101

    Increasing corporate value with sustainability 105
Rethinking the economy **111**
    Post-growth equals zero growth 113
    Social performance instead of Material throughput 116
    Efficiency-consistency-sufficiency 121
    Fundamentals of the economy of tomorrow 127
    Sustainable Finance 131
It doesn't work without change **139**
    Who is joining in? 139
    False role model 144
Closing remarks **147**
Acknowledgement **151**
About the author **153**
About the Diplomatic Council **155**
Books from DC Publishing **157**
Bibliography **159**
References and Notes **161**

Foreword

We were sitting on the terrace of the small café of the former Herrenmühle. The Kinzig rushed over the weir with a loud roar so that you could barely hear your own words. Severe weather had hit Germany in the last few days. Masses of rain had washed away entire houses, devastated villages, turned streets into raging rivers; dams collapsed under the masses of water.

The flood of the century caused over 170 deaths and destroyed countless livelihoods. The damage totalled more than 12 billion euros. The Kinzig was also filled to the high banks. The news and talk shows had no other topic for days. The consequences of climate change had now also become brutally visible on our doorstep. Our conversation involuntarily led us from the increasing natural disasters worldwide to the ongoing Covid-19 pandemic to the importance of sustainability and the limited natural resources on our planet.

"These topics have been on my mind for quite a while. I've finally found someone I can share my thoughts with," said my dialogue partner happily. How can we constantly increase our economic output and boost our consumption, even though the necessary global resources are limited and diminishing year on year? Can we continue to accept that forests are being cleared on an enormous scale and animal and plant species are being wiped out just to satisfy our hunger for consumption? How long can we keep the people of the so-called "Third World", who produce our haute couture for low wages and under sometimes unsocial conditions, in their home countries and prevent them from taking a slice of the prosperity cake?

We quickly had to admit to ourselves that we ourselves are part of the causal system and that a solution is only possible by changing our own consumer behaviour. In the light of our discussions, the arguments of Fridays for Future and Scientist for Future no longer seemed so radical. On the contrary, it seems that only compelling demands can bring about a gradual change in society.

It is almost a truism that we cannot continue to grow indefinitely on our planet with only limited resources. Nevertheless, after centuries of growth and the incomparable economic miracle after the Second World War, we find it difficult to say goodbye to our cherished consumer habits. But it is almost certain that we will have no other choice in the future.

It has taken 50 years and a pandemic for the findings of Donella and Dennis Meadows in their study on the state of humanity and the future of the global economy regarding the limits of our actions to become part of everyday political and social life.[1]

Foreword

The predicted climate change is happening and can no longer be denied. The consequences of the progressive, accelerating overexploitation of our ecosystem's capacity are becoming increasingly visible.

We are robbing ourselves of our own livelihood with our eyes wide open.

"The key question is: how do we convince enough people on all continents to seriously address this issue and bring their social and economic systems into balance with the Earth's ecosystem?" my counterpart concluded.

A 15-year-old girl has made government and corporate leaders sit up and take notice. Greta Thunberg has managed to get the world to listen to her and set a movement in motion that has made people all over the world think.

We have reached red alert level, warned António Guterres, Secretary-General of the United Nations, in his speech in Malaysia on 18 April 2021 in view of the inadequate plans to limit global warming by all 193 member states.[2]

We have to make the right decisions *today* for our lives tomorrow.

Helmut von Siedmogrodzki

Time for a paradigm shift

Forests the size of Sicily are burning in Russia, natural disasters are occurring one after the other with ever more devastating consequences, our fish stocks are contaminated with antibiotics and microplastics, animal and plant species are dying out on a massive scale and drinking water is becoming an increasingly scarce commodity. These and similar events are the consequences of the unchecked overexploitation of natural resources and mindless mass consumption. Our economic model is geared towards growth - not only in capitalism, even in communist China. Without growth, there is no employment, no investment, no innovation and no prosperity - that is the dogma. But where do we want to grow to and for how long? It is an undisputed realisation that endless growth is simply impossible with finite resources.

"Anyone who believes that exponential growth could go on indefinitely in a finite world is either a madman or an economist." (Kenneth Boulding at a hearing of the US Congress in 1973).[3]

With a world population expected to reach 9.7 billion people in 2050, our ecosystem is likely to reach its limits if per capita income growth rates and consumer behaviour remain unchanged.

At the end of 2015, 193 member states of the United Nations adopted the "2030 Agenda for Sustainable Development" with 17 Sustainable Development Goals (SDGs). The agenda aims to end poverty, protect the planet and achieve prosperity for all. But what does prosperity mean? And does prosperity go hand in hand with greater satisfaction? The fact is that the catalogue of goods that count as basic needs has grown steadily in affluent countries, but satisfaction has declined in relative terms.[4] Several studies show that the increase in life satisfaction not only stops increasing above a certain income level, but actually decreases sharply.[5]

This may explain the growing disenchantment with politics and dissatisfaction with living conditions, self-doubt and mistrust of governments in western industrialised countries, especially in times of crisis such as the coronavirus pandemic.

Urbanisation has brought more and more people together in anonymous blocks of flats and at the same time distanced us from nature. We want an egg for breakfast but complain about the annoying cockcrow. Digitalisation is doing the rest to remove us from the rhythm of natural time sequences. The consequences are social poverty, aggression and permanent stress situations. In this living environment, increasing dissatisfaction is making its way in the form of violent visitors to football stadiums, stone-throwing, aggressive demonstrators and attacks on innocent citizens.

Land-grabbing cities and the progressive destruction of flora and fauna habitats are narrowing the communities of humans and wild animals. This in turn favours the transmission of viruses from animals to humans and promotes the spread of pandemics such as Covid-19 or Ebola.

Continued growth will (perhaps) ultimately bring us a higher standard of living, but not more life satisfaction. Unchecked growth is exhausting ourselves and our ecosystem. In large parts of the world, living conditions will deteriorate dramatically and jeopardise this very prosperity. A paradigm shift in the organisation of our economic system and our understanding of prosperity is necessary.

Limits to growth

The authors of the 1972 Club of Rome study "Limits to Growth" already came to the conclusion that a paradigm shift was necessary, and many of the assumptions and findings have been confirmed in various subsequent studies and the current development of climate change.[6]

In particular, their statement that the outgoing winds from ruminants contribute significantly to global warming, namely through the methane gas released, was more likely to provoke laughter than serious discussion. In the meantime, this result has also become a fact.

Tim Jackson, British economist and professor of sustainable development, showed a way out of the "growth dilemma" in his updated work "Prosperity without growth - the update" (2017): Moving away from a materialistic, excessive consumerism that encourages us to buy a new smartphone every six months, the latest fashion and a new fancy car every three years, towards a service-orientated market economy that provides us with the goods we need and want to shape our lives.

The focus of this economic and social system is no longer on status symbols, such as the biggest and fastest car, the most expensive flat, the smartest outfit, financial success and image, but on self-acceptance, relationships and belonging to a community. "People who orientate themselves more towards these inner values are happier and at the same time feel more responsible for the environment than People with materialistic values," says Tim Kasser, Professor of Psychology at Knox College in Illinois.[7] He has been researching values and well-being for years with many renowned colleagues and is known for his studies on the negative effects of materialism.[8] "Turning to people's 'inner values' instead of emphasising outward appearances makes them happier and improves their quality of life." - These are the conclusions of a study conducted by Professor Helga Dittmar and colleagues in 2014.[9]

The Growth Mantra

Since the industrial revolution in the 19th century, countries, particularly in the western hemisphere with ist market economy, have experienced incredible economic growth. This growth scenario has been accompanied by technological advances at ever shorter intervals. Although there have also been setbacks during the last 100 years, economic crises, the Great Depression, hyperinflation and wars. However, fueling the arms industry only delayed the economic collapse, but did not prevent it. After the Second World War, almost all industrialised countries were more or less back to square one. This was particularly true for Germany. The reconstruction of Germany and other countries involved in the Second World War was driven by the irrepressible will to get the economy up and running again, create jobs and generate prosperity. This worked wonderfully with generous financial injections from the USA (the "Marshall Plan"), monetary reform and creative entrepreneurship. Year after year, wages rose, working hours were reduced and prosperity steadily increased for more and more people, supported by a steady increase in economic growth. However, despite the high level of prosperity achieved for the general public, trade unions continue to demand higher wages and salaries, while company owners want higher profits, which are secured through higher productivity and cost reductions on the one hand and price increases on the other.

The managers of corporations subordinate themselves to the shareholders' demand to constantly increase the company value of the investment. Cost-cutting programmes replace one another, employees are laid off, which in turn reduces general purchasing power. Where will this spiral of continuous growth lead?

The financial crisis of 2007/08 revealed the fragility of this economic system. A worldwide collapse of the financial system and the global economy was only prevented by immense financial injections and a still hungry China. The early collapse of our financial and economic system was postponed by a huge accumulation of debt. Once again, the mantra was that the economy must grow in order to maintain employment and prosperity. The financial crisis could have been a warning, an opportunity for a path to reorientation, but instead this warning went largely unheeded.

The coronavirus pandemic has done nothing to change this. The broad social discourse triggered by the measures to combat the pandemic mainly centred on the rights of the individual. First and foremost, civil liberties. In contrast, climate protection and the depletion of natural resources through insatiable consumption took a back seat. But without nature, there can be no freedom. What civil liberties remain to us when arable land becomes desolate, areas of land sink into the sea, poverty rises in developing countries and trigger an unimagined migration of peoples? Even during the pandemic, there were renewed calls for the growth of the slowed-down global economy.

According to the Institute of International Finance (IIF), global debt has risen by 87 trillion dollars to over 322 per cent of global gross domestic product since the 2008 financial crisis. In order to iron out the dent in the economic performance of its member states caused by coronavirus, the European Union has decided to set up a coronavirus recovery fund totalling 750 billion euros, which - how else? - will be financed by loans. US President Joe Biden even launched a 2.2 trillion dollar programme. The Federal Reserve of the United States of America was afraid to raise the interest rate, which would drive many countries into insolvency and could trigger a second global financial and economic crisis. We are our own prisoners of the growth mantra.

Society in transition

We live in disruptive times. Technological development is progressing at a breathtaking pace, leaving most of us unsettled. Artificial intelligence, blockchain, the Internet of Things and quantum computers can only be grasped using abstract mathematical formulas and remain a closed book for the general public. Our behaviour is determined by algorithms.

The mass processing of our personal data by market-dominating corporations that provide us with our daily, predicted wishes convey a feeling of manipulation, of no longer being able to determine one's own actions. This feeling of powerlessness is increasingly being countered by the desire for change. Young people in particular are drawing attention to themselves and emphatically formulating their demands for a new social consensus. This consensus calls for an economic sustainability model that is in harmony with the overall ecological system of the earth's satellite.

The limits to growth are defined by the sustainability and re-availability of resources and compatibility with the ecosystem that makes our lives possible. The consequences of the largely undisputed, negative climate change, the progressive extinction of animal and plant species, the increase in natural disasters and pandemics are already clearly visible today and set the limits for future action. While technological progress is rushing past us like a high-speed train, the changes to our ecosystem have so far only been apparent at longer intervals, like a snail's pace. This slowness across generations makes it difficult for us to recognise and understand the need to change our behaviour as consumers and economic agents. However, without adapting to the conditions created, the change in our ecosystem - and thus the negative consequences - is also likely to accelerate.

There is no doubt that the challenge we face is enormous. Nothing less is required than to break with centuries-old paradigms. Our entire prosperity is based on the assumption of continuous growth, fuelled by constant innovation. So how can we maintain the prosperity achieved of the industrialised countries on the one hand, and yet with the world population increasing and the less developed regions having to catch up on huge demand, how can we achieve a balance between consumption and supply of available basic commodities and nutrients, while maintaining social peace?

Growth and socio-ecological balance

The massive impact of our economic activities on the global ecosystem of our planet has already thrown it significantly out of balance and is already overtaxing nature's ability to regenerate in parts. On the other hand, just how quickly the environment can recover can be seen, for example, in the growth of fish stocks in otherwise overfished waters that were left alone during the coronavirus pandemic.

Politicians, environmental organisations and scientists are therefore pursuing the "decoupling" approach. Continued growth should be made possible through more efficient production processes, the increased use of renewable raw materials, the reduced use of materials, the reduction of emissions and innovative and environmentally friendly products. The German government also focused on "decoupling" in its 2021 sustainability strategy. But do growth and decoupling really lead to a balance in the natural habitat and the mitigation of the consequences of climate change?

Growth and prosperity cannot only apply to the western industrialised nations. The 193 member states of the United Nations have pledged to eradicate poverty and hunger worldwide by 2030. We are miles away from this goal. At the same time, we in the Western Hemisphere produce food in abundance. As if that were not enough, we are wasting food and new products that have not found a buyer for the sake of price stability and growth - an absurdity! The wealth gap in our societies at home and around the world has now grown to a level that inevitably fuels social unrest. The flow of refugees to Europe or from Central America to the United States of America is just a small foretaste of the expected movements of peoples and the social conflicts that will accompany them.

Millions of people have been living in fenced-in refugee camps for decades with no hope of ever escaping this fringe of civilisation. Economic systems geared towards growth will further exacerbate this situation. Urbanisation and the associated sealing of arable land, the mass clearing of forests, the destruction of the habitats of diverse animal and plant species and the exploitation of the earth's natural resources have developed a momentum of their own, acting as a catalyst to accelerate climate change and the destruction of our habitat.

During his time as Finance Minister of the Federal Republic of Germany in 2021, Olaf Scholz emphasised the seriousness of the situation: "We need a second industrial revolution in order to achieve the climate targets and maintain our prosperity." He continued: "If we fail to do this now, we will jeopardise our industry, our jobs and our prosperity."[10]

The German Chancellor at the time, Angela Merkel, also issued a warning, "the implementation of the sustainability goals cannot be achieved at the current pace."[11]

At their sustainability summit in 2019, the member states of the United Nations postulated that the Sustainable Development Goals would not be achieved in 2030 if current trends continue. Climate change, species extinction and rising resource consumption are just as obviously reaching planetary limits as questions of justice between generations and regions are in need of a solution.[12]

At his second swearing-in ceremony as Secretary-General of the United Nations, António Guterres emphasised to the assembled ambassadors: „We are truly at a crossroads, with consequential choices before us. Paradigms are shifting. Old orthodoxies are being flipped."

But how is anything supposed to change when influencers suggest to us every day that we need a new car, youthful cosmetics, new clothes, a new smartphone, a bigger house and all of this super cheap, cheapest, for almost no money? The coronavirus crisis has also made us realise that these products can no longer be produced at such low prices in this country. Even China is already considered too expensive by many companies after wages and social security contributions have been raised by an average of more than ten per cent annually for decades. Since the invention of the discounter, our society has developed into an "I-want-everything-but-cheap" community. While in the early days of the discounter era, people looked down on the less well-off customers of the new competitors, today the Porsche and Mercedes drivers are not afraid to browse the shelves of discount retailers. Only those who spend little stay rich!

Can our social and economic system only survive if we have a generous pay rise in our pockets every year, if the dividends for shareholders are increased every year, and if the salaries of star company executives are in the hundreds of millions? Do football players have to collect million-dollar salaries while children in Bangladesh sew their jerseys for just a few cents? In the end, we all pay the price.

We are at a crossroads, said António Guterres. The necessary changes ahead of us may seem as utopian as the abandonment of horse-drawn carriages in the 19th century and their replacement by autonomous vehicles in the 21st century. Today's Generation Z will unlikely ever play car quartet cards where the most cylinders and highest horsepower wins. These descendants will only experience the adrenaline rush of the gas pedal of a 600-horsepower bolide in a motordrome. Self-driving, comfortably equipped communication vehicles that are available on demand in just a few minutes will take people to their destinations in the future without any noise or emissions. The car, long time a status symbol, is returning to its original purpose: transportation.

The decade of action

Decoupling and disruptive technologies alone will not be enough to preserve our living spaces. We must fundamentally change our behaviour and our economic system. However, this does not necessarily have to happen at the expense of reasonable prosperity. However, we can expect general satisfaction to increase again the lower our materialistic demands are. Many studies and research findings prove that such an economic and social system is possible.

On the other hand, "business as usual" will inevitably lead to the planetary limits and thus also jeopardise our economic prosperity. Prof. Thomas Döring from Darmstadt University of

Applied Sciences painted an even gloomier picture in an article in the July 2019 issue of *Wirtschaftsdienst* (journal for economic policy): "The intensity with which economic activity is now intervening in natural control cycles could jeopardise the continued existence of human civilisation itself."[13]

Politicians around the world have long recognised the urgency of taking action. Only the way forward is a matter of debate. The United Nations has proclaimed the current decade as the "Decade of Action and Delivery for Sustainable Development". The drive for action is primarily based on the goal of slowing down climate change and achieving CO_2 neutrality by 2050. By 2030 - in far less than ten years! - all countries in the world together would have to reduce greenhouse gas emissions by at least 45 per cent compared to 2010. At the climate summit in September 2019, the Secretary-General of the United Nations commented on the plans presented by the member states: *"But so far, those plans achieve less than a one per cent cut in emissions. This is a true red alert for people and planet."*

The Ruhr region, a former backbone of Germany's industry, has had 25 years to say goodbye to coal mining and turn to new technologies. Nature will hardly give us that much time. We are approaching the "point of no return" with increasing speed. In other words, the point at which all our measures to slow down global warming, halt the extinction of species and preserve habitats will no longer be effective. Then we will inevitably be exposed to catastrophes of unimagined proportions.

The mammoth task ahead of us can only be accomplished together with all countries in the global community. All levels of society must contribute to this. We are talking about nothing less than a quantum leap in our social and economic system. So let's think about what well-being and satisfaction really mean to us. It seems that we no longer have a choice anyway.

Living in abudance

The throwaway society

After the Second World War, Europe, especially the Western allies, but also some economic powers in the East, for example Japan followed by South Korea, experienced an unrivalled economic boom. The post-war boom was made possible by an unprecedented stimulus package totalling 13.12 billion US dollars, named after the then US Secretary of State George C. Marshall, the "Marshall Plan" (equivalent to more than 140 billion US dollars in 2020).

The economic rise was accompanied by increasingly rapid technological development. In this positive, promising environment, the assumption probably also grew that prosperity only knew one direction: upwards. There have been a few setbacks in the meantime, such as the 1973 oil crisis, the dot.com bubble and the 2008 financial crisis, to name but a few. But none of these events have been able to diminish the unshakeable belief in the continued development of prosperity, accompanied by unbroken confidence in technological progress.

Politicians, investors and analysts continue to pressurize entrepreneurs to keep growing, to tap into new markets and to constantly increase profits. If these expectations are not met, listed companies lose a considerable proportion of their enterprise value within no time. Skilful, manipulative marketing is constantly generating new demand. The holding time of a classic phone has been reduced from years to less than a year with the next generation of "smart phones". Washing machines, fridges and other so-called white goods that used to last ten to 15 years in a household are being replaced in half the time with the promise of better, more economical technology. Every four months, the fashion industry presents us with a new collection of clothes that we absolutely have to buy in order to stay "trendy". Overproduction and stock is either destroyed or thrown onto the market far below the original price. The author remembers how customers stormed into the Alster departmentstores' in Hamburg in 1976 for the summer and winter sales and snatched the reduced goods out of each other's hands. This hunting instinct among shoppers has not changed to this day.

Cheap is the trend. Since the invention of the discounter in retail, marketing is no longer conceivable without the key words "cheap", "discount", "reduced" or "affordable". The "Deal of the day", "Black Friday" and "Cybersale" announce the sale of previously high-priced goods and services at unbeatably low prices, causing even the most modest consumer to lose their last inhibitions. The cheap Jacob at the fish market in Hamburg couldn't do better. Initially, retail shops resembling warehouses, where bulk goods were sold in open boxes on simple shelves, were associated with low product quality (no branded goods). Only those on low incomes shopped there. Today, even the affluent clientele are not afraid to drive up in their Mercedes or Porsche to buy their household needs at a favourable price. The principle of mass sales with high turnover has found many imitators. Furniture, shoes, photos and clothing are sold en masse according to the discount principle. Competitors undercut each other every week with ever new special offers and encourage increased consumption. The slogan "Buy 3 for the price of 2" encourages some customers to buy even though they only need small quantities. Where the goods come from, how sustainably the products were made and how you manage to sell a T-shirt for five euros that was sewn in Sri Lanka or Bangladesh is hardly questioned. Dollar Tree, an American company that sells its goods for a dollar, can hardly save itself from sales and profit growth. Investors are rewarded with continuously rising share prices of the company, which is traded on the NASDAQ.

The consumer society of modern times has developed into an overflow and throwaway society. Defective appliances or broken items of clothing are simply disposed of and replaced with a new item; repairs are more expensive nowadays. According to research by Greenpeace, supported by investigations by the German TV magazine *Frontal21* and *Wirtschaftswoche*, Amazon Europe destroys new goods and returns in mint condition, from T-shirts to electrical goods, preferably at top-secret locations in Belgium and Germany instead of blocking expensive storage capacity with slow-moving stock.[14] Video footage from Greenpeace and Panorama shows how new goods and returns packaged ready for sale are destroyed in the hidden warehouses and then disposed of as waste. The destruction and disposal of new goods has been banned in Germany since 2020. However, as of the publication of this book, a legal ordinance that actually enforces the ban is still missing.

The appreciation of the objects we consume has been lost. Amazon is just one example that shows how thoughtlessly we consume in the modern world. The fact that this behaviour is causing lasting damage to our environment and depriving us of our livelihoods in the long term is still largely ignored, despite years of warnings from scientists.

Wrong incentives

Misguided subsidy policies have contributed to the overproduction of food in developed industrialised countries for decades. In the 1950s, a subsidy policy was introduced to boost agricultural production in the still young European Economic Community, which led to the famous "butter mountain" 20 years later. Accustomed to the state-guaranteed prices, farmers invested significantly more in grain and livestock than the market demanded. The result: in the 1970s, the production of milk, meat and grain significantly exceeded demand. The surplus butter was stored by the state in the countries of the EEC[1].

---

[1] The EEC = European Economic Community was the forerunner of today's European Union and was founded in 1957 with the signing of the Treaty of Rome by France, Italy, the Federal Republic of Germany, Belgium, the Netherlands and Luxembourg.

Only at Christmas time were stocks offered at reduced prices in the retail trade. It would take until 2007 to empty the stocks.[15]

In 1992, the EEC states began to take countermeasures by paying farmers to set aside land. These state interventions cost taxpayers billions. Nevertheless, volume control has still not been successful. The so-called "pig cycle", which describes how the balance between supply and demand is regulated by the market price of a commodity, was cancelled out by the subsidy policy. The state interventions were no coincidence: the state wanted to ensure the supply of food for its citizens and at the same time provide farmers with a sufficient income.

The agreements on the European Union's Common Agricultural Policy (CAP) continue to lead to surplus production that is not orientated towards demand. Excessive livestock populations pollute our drinking water by overfertilizing the land with liquid manure and contribute significantly to the increase in greenhouse gases through the methane emissions of the animals. Methane gases have been proven to be a major contributor to global warming. In addition to liquid manure, enormous quantities of pesticides are used to secure the harvest and contaminate our soils in the long term. Between 2000 and 2012, the global use of pesticides increased by 36 per cent to 4.2 million tonnes. While the use of chemicals in Europe is declining slightly, the total amount used worldwide has levelled off at the 2012 level. Asia and therefore China (42 per cent share of consumption alone) and America are among the largest users of pesticides.[16]

The increase in productivity is reaching its natural limits due to soil leaching. Where there are not enough natural fertilisers available, inorganic chemicals are used. In 2019, the consumption of inorganic fertilisers amounted to 189 million tonnes - an increase of 40 per cent compared to the year 2000. In the same period the world population only increased by 26%. The main consumers of non-organic fertilisers are China, India, the USA and Brazil. Africa recorded the largest increase in the period mentioned, with a growth rate of 79 per cent, albeit still at a very low level of three million tonnes. With the use of 351 kilograms of nitrogen, phosphorus and potassium per hectare of cultivated land, China also stands out within Asia, which averages 180 kilograms per hectare overall. Only countries in the Middle East, such as Kuwait, Bahrain and Egypt, use far more of these chemicals per hectare of cultivated land in order to provide the soil with sufficient nutrients. The downside of this excessive nutrient supply is the pollution of drinking water with the nitrogen compound nitrate and the emission of nitrous oxide, which also contributes significantly to global warming.[17] Germany has been criticised for years for failing to comply with the EU-wide limit value for nitrates of 50 milligrams per litre. In the period from 2016 to 2018, the nitrate value was over 90 milligrams per litre at around 27 per cent of all 692 measuring-points set up nationwide. Only just under half of the measuring points have recorded a value below 25 milligrams per litre, almost unchanged since 2012.[18]

On 28 July 2022, all of the Earth's resources that can be regenerated in one year were used up. In terms of the year, the world's population would have to have 1.75 Earths to cover the demand for basic materials. In 1972, the threshold date was still 14 December. At that time, the world was still almost in order.[19]

According to the Food and Agriculture Organisation of the United Nations (FAO), 14 per cent of the food produced worldwide is lost every year on its way from harvest to the food retailer.[20] A further 17 per cent is thrown away by retailers and consumers (UNEP 2021).[21] Overall, a third of all food is lost on its way from harvest to plate. At the same time, despite all efforts, the number of people suffering from hunger has risen since 2015 to more than 760 million in 2021.[22] According to the FAO's 2022 report, the proportion of hungry people in Africa rose to over 20 per cent in 2021, the same percentage as 17 years earlier in 2005. This corresponds to almost 280 million Africans. In terms of numbers, this is only surpassed by Asia with more than 420 million hungry people. How long do we think this imbalance will last before people migrate to places where there is enough food, namely Europe, America and China?

Fight for the habitats

The migration of people has long since begun. People from Latin America have been immigrating illegally to the United States of America for decades. They expect better living conditions there than in their home countries. During his time as President of the USA, Donald Trump tried to protect the country from immigrants with walls and steel fences. In Europe, too, we are seeing defence reactions towards people who leave their country because of hunger or war and expect blooming meadows in the golden west. Frontex, the European Border and Coast Guard Agency, was further expanded in 2016. Its tasks were expanded from the mere control of migration flows to border protection.[23]

In 2021, almost 200,000 people attempted to immigrate to Europe illegally. Mostly from crisis areas such as Syria and Afghanistan, but also from Tunisia, Morocco and Algeria.[24] The refugee flows are also being instrumentalised politically. For example, Belarus under dictator Alexander Lukashenko is accused of allowing migrants to fly into Belarus and smuggling them illegally to Western Europe via Poland or the Balkan states. To protect against being "flooded" by migrants, the EU countries have reached an agreement with Turkey. Turkey is holding around 3.8 million people in camps (as of 2021), thereby preventing them from immigrating to EU member states. According to the 2021 annual report of the United Nations Refugee Agency (UNHCR), this camp is the largest in the world.

According to the annual UNHCR report, 89.3 million people worldwide were displaced at the end of 2021. This is the highest number of refugees since the Second World War; it is twice as high as ten years earlier.[25] The UNHCR estimates that the number of people displaced from their homes will already exceed 100 million in 2022. In addition to the refugee movements caused by power struggles and historical conflicts, the fight for food and resources is expected to lead to a tens of times higher migration in the coming decades.

The archipelago of Tuvalu makes it into the headlines of the news agencies on 10 November 2023. The island state in the Pacific Ocean is home to around 11,500 inhabitants on nine islands. The Commonwealth member could become the first victim of continuously rising sea levels in less than 100 years. The highest point in the archipelago is now only five meters above sea level. Australia has declared its willingness to take in the climate asylum seekers.[26]

In 2015, when war refugees and displaced persons from Syria poured into the EU and Germany in particular, the majority of the population's mood was still characterised by "We can do it" under former German Chancellor Angela Merkel. Eight years later and one year after Russia's invasion of Ukraine, the mood has reached a tipping point. Local authorities are groaning under the burden of the influx of asylum seekers and refugees. Countries such as Hungary and Poland refused to take in migrants as early as 2015.

At the EU summit in June 2023, Hungary's Prime Minister Viktor Orban already spoke of a "fight for freedom" against EU asylum policy and a "migration war" in relation to the debate on the distribution of asylum seekers and refugees among the member states.[27] Cyprus is barely able to cope with the growing influx of illegal immigrants from Syria, Nigeria and Turkey. 60 per cent of refugees not entitled to asylum who seek their fortune via the eastern Mediterranean route end up in Cyprus.[28] In Germany, Italy, France and other EU member states, calls to limit the intake of asylum seekers and refugees are becoming ever louder. Politicians of all colours feel compelled to act if they do not want to lose their voters and prevent the clearly perceptible resentment among the population from erupting.

In September 2020, the European Commission proposed a new migration and asylum package to the European Parliament in order not to jeopardise the cohesion of the member states. At its core, it was about strengthening the EU's external borders, combating unauthorised entry through a screening procedure at the external borders, the possible implementation of Asylum procedures in third countries - which are of course remunerated for this - so that unauthorised persons do not even make the life-threatening journey to the EU - so the hope, the definition of a larger number of so-called safe countries of origin and the more effective return of migrants without right of residence to these countries.[29]

In April 2023, the Parliament agreed on a new regulation for a new asylum and migration pact and was now ready to start negotiations with the Council.[30] In April 2024, the EU Parliament approved the reform of the common asylum system by a majority. However, many parliamentarians share the concern that climate refugees will increasingly seek their way into EU member states in the coming years in addition to politically persecuted and war- displaced persons. It is to be feared that the last humanitarian and solidary inhibitions will then also fall in favour of their own well-being.

Stopping global warming and therefore curbing the increase in natural disasters and the destruction of arable land, as well as securing food supplies in the world's vulnerable areas, is an essential prerequisite for preventing the refugee scenario described above.

In recognition of the effects of climate change, the 154 participating countries decided at the 2023 climate conference in Dubai to set up a fund to compensate the poorer countries, most of which were affected through no fault of their own, for losses and damage. The 700 million US dollars initially pledged during the conference are a drop in the ocean compared to the already agreed annual 100 billion dollars that the member states consider necessary for measures to limit global warming and combat the effects of climate change.

The 2023 World Climate Conference has highlighted the displeasure of the suffering countries of Africa and Asia at the lack of progress made by the major economic powers and main sources of greenhouse gas emissions. Money alone will not eradicate the damage caused and the increasing consequences for these population groups.

We need to readjust our behaviour, our attitude to consumption and to the values of wealth, success, happiness and satisfaction. It is obvious that this will not be easy for us. However, we have already exceeded the limits of what this planet Earth provides us with as a basis for life. Acting together and rethinking our economic principles is the order of the day. Sustainability and environmentally friendly action must be at the centre of this new economic and social model.

Growth on Credit

The financing of larger purchases by means of a loan has a long tradition. The first lending transactions are documented more than 5,000 years ago.[31] Farmers borrowed seed and repaid their debts after the harvest by returning new seed plus a quantity premium as interest. The investment loan was born. A risky business for the borrower. Only if favourable weather conditions brought a rich harvest was the farmer able to service his loan. All too often, the loan did not work out and the farmer lost his possessions. Emperors, kings and governments financed and still finance wars and their political visions through loans. State investments play an important role in the economic system. If taxes are not sufficient, high-interest government bonds are issued to finance a project. Borrowing money is as familiar to us as the shirt and trousers we put on every day.

Since the invention of instalment credit, we have become accustomed to purchasing the object of our desire when we do not yet have the necessary financial means. Buy now, pay later. In 1807, the oldest furniture store in the USA at the time, Cowperthwait & Sons, introduced the purchase of an item using a payment plan in New York City.[32] The idea of allowing the buyer to pay for the product in regular instalments over a certain period of time was a clever marketing decision. Boosting sales in this way quickly found imitators and is now an integral part of business life. Whether large or small wishes, nowadays, everything can be done by paying in installments. However, some people fall into the debt trap when the income that has been factored in is cancelled or is significantly lower than expected. Consumer credit, with all its facets, is very closely linked to the idea of growth in economic systems. Between 1991 and 2022, loans granted to private individuals in Germany alone more than tripled to just under 1,495.8 billion euros or almost 1.5 trillion euros.[33] According to Statista, consumer spending by private households totalled 1.92 trillion euros in 2022.[34] Germany's gross domestic product as a measure of the goods and services produced in a year has only slightly more than doubled in nominal terms in the same period from just under 1.6 trillion euros (1991) to almost 3.9 trillion euros (2022), but only increased 1.4 times in price-adjusted terms.[35] In 2022, 38.6 per cent of GDP was therefore financed by private loans.

Generally speaking, taking out a loan is not something to be criticised. Research and development of companies often swallow up sums in the billions, which can only be recouped after several years. As was the case 5,000 years ago, the granting of microloans in poorer countries has enabled the local population to create their own livelihoods and jobs. Countries regularly finance their large-scale projects and households by issuing ten- to 30-year bonds, which, according to the general assessment, provide investors with a secure and regular additional income. It becomes critical when borrowing gets out of hand and we cannot expect that the borrowed capital can ever be repaid. This is the situation we find ourselves in today.

The debt trap

In November 2023, Germany's Federal Constitutional Court declared the reclassification of a loan totalling 60 billion euros, which was taken out by the government in 2021 for additional expenditure during the coronavirus pandemic as an emergency requirement (for this purpose, the debt brake had been suspended), as a fund for regular climate protection measures to be unconstitutional. This was an unprecedented blow in the history of the Federal Republic of Germany

The Federal Constitutional Court saw the misuse of the loan as a violation of the exception to the debt brake in emergency situations provided for in the law.[36] The Federal Constitutional Court saw the misuse of the loan as a violation of the exception to the debt brake in emergency situations provided for in the law.36 The latter does not include regular expenditure in the federal budget and therefore does not include the financing of planned climate protection programmes and the transfer of the emergency loan to a climate and transformation fund, which is not part of the federal budget but was created as a special fund and secondary budget. To combat the corona pandemic, the federal government had to take out loans that exceeded the debt brake by a total of 240 billion euros. 60 billion euros were ultimately not needed and were instead supposed to flow into projects to accelerate the energy transition, which were now sorely lacking.

The creation of special funds is certainly possible under the Basic Law of the Federal Republic of Germany. However, these must be clearly defined in terms of their purpose and scope, not be able to be fulfilled efficiently from the core budget and be an exception.[37] In fact, according to the report of the Federal Audit Office, the German federal government is managing 29 special funds in 2023 - many of them with their own credit authorisation.[38] The aforementioned judgement reinforces the Federal Court of Auditors' view that the creation of special funds dilutes the transparency of the core budget, which is much more in the focus of parliament and the public, and that circumventing the debt brake is not a trivial offence. With the Second Supplementary Budget Act 2021, the federal government also attempted in 2022 to create more financial leeway for future years, especially for the transformation to a climate-neutral economy, by exploiting the emergency clause and undermining the debt rule through a new accounting practice in future budget periods. The Federal Constitutional Court rejected this approach, which had been approved by the majority of the German Bundestag, and declared it unconstitutional. With significant consequences for budget planning from 2024.

The term special assets itself is already misleading, as the vast majority of ancillary budgets, totalling 780 billion euros, are loan-financed.[39] Until 2009, special assets were a way for clever finance ministers to circumvent the so-called "golden rule". This stipulated that the net borrowing of the federal government could not exceed the sum of the investments budgeted in the budget. The directive provided an exception for special budgets and, according to Reischmann[40] provided an incentive for the federal and state governments to take on debt outside their core budgets.[2] While the public usually focuses on budget deficits, it tends to go unnoticed that the new debt of a budget period often goes far beyond this, namely via the special budgets. This limits the transparency of government debt.[41] In its report of 25 August 2023 regarding the special funds, the Federal Audit Office criticises the fact that their unused credit authorisations at the end of 2022, at around 522 billion euros, are five times the borrowing reported in the financial planning period 2023 to 2027. The concealment of the actual net borrowing (NCA) becomes clear when comparing the NCA shown in the budget plans including the special budgets. While the 2023 budget only shows new borrowing of 45.6 billion euros, the NCA including the special budgets is 192.8 billion euros. That is a deviation of over 422 per cent. In 2022, the Federal Audit Office estimated the deviation at over 69 per cent.

The Federal Audit Office warns: "The budget-volatile expenditure and its equally budget-volatile credit financing endanger the parliamentary budgetary right and the effectiveness of the

---

[2] This practice was abolished with the introduction of a debt ceiling – 0,35% of nominal GDP – in 2010.

debt rule. Parliament (but also the public) is in danger of losing the overview and thus also the control."

Since the records of the Federal Statistical Office, Germany's total debt has increased more than 250-fold from 9.6 billion euros in 1950 to 2,408,626,000,000 euros (2.4 trillion euros) in June 2023. The federal government's share of total debt has grown from 35 per cent initially to 69 per cent in 2023. The state is increasingly intervening in the economy with ever new investment and economic stimulus programmes, which also conceal election gifts from the ruling parties to their clientele. The federal states and municipalities have also run up massive debts since the post-war period: from 6.1 billion euros in 1950 to 594.4 billion euros as at June 2023 (federal states) and 0.1 billion euros to 144.7 billion (municipalities). Until 2012, the debt of public budgets rose steadily. In particular, the financial burdens following Germany's reunification from 1990 to 1995 and the financial crisis of 2008/2009 were challenging events that were reflected in the level of debt. From 2013 onwards, the German government began to reduce debt through repayment. With the outbreak of the coronavirus pandemic, these efforts came to an end. Around 170 billion euros in debt reduction was overcompensated by a further 509 billion euros in loans by 2023. As a result, the debt rule under Article 109(3) of the German Basic Law was suspended in the years 2020 to 2022 due to the special emergency situation. Despite the attempt to achieve balanced budgets in the medium-term planning for 2024 to

2027, the debt mountain of the federal government alone is set to grow by EUR 63 billion (according to the BMF's budget planning)[3]; according to the Ministry of Finance's projection, this will then amount to 65.5 per cent of the price adjusted gross domestic product. 5.5 per cent above the convergence criterion of the Maastricht Treaty.[4]

While a not insignificant number of politicians and experts in light of emerging recession fears in 2023 call for further state investment and a renewed suspension of the debt rule, governments are sacrificing their ability to act in the future. Not only will the debt have to be repaid one day at the expense of future budgets, but the interest payments will also not be available for other important tasks. After more than ten years of low interest rates, during which the German state - and other countries - could easily borrow at zero per cent interest, interest rates in Europe have already risen to over three per cent. Interest payments, which had fallen to 3.9 billion euros in 2021 with a 0.71 percent share of the total budget, already amounted to 15.3 billion euros again in 2022 (3.2 percent of the total budget) and

---

[3] We have already pointed out the reduced informative value due to the inadequate consideration of the financing requirements for the special assets.

[4] The convergence criteria of the Maastricht Agreement stipulate that the overall economic deficit of a member state may not exceed three per cent of gross domestic product per year. Furthermore, the debt level of the member state should not exceed the limit of 60 per cent of its own gross domestic product. Until the coronavirus crisis in 2020, Germany was on a stable path of debt reduction and in 2019 met the Maastricht debt criterion for the first time since 2002.

were ten times higher in the 2023 budget with an expected 39.9 billion euros.[42] This makes the item the fourth highest in the 2023 federal budget, almost on a par with spending on general financial administration, after social and defence spending and almost twice as high as spending on education and research.

In the years from 2028, this item will increase significantly, namely by the statutory amortisation payments of the borrowings from 2020 to 2022 and the special assets. As the second largest budget item, annuities will also exceed the defence budget. Regular tasks are already barely manageable, as school buildings in need of renovation, a dilapidated rail network and motorway bridges in danger of collapsing show us every day.

During the writing of this chapter, the media reported that, as a result of the Constitutional Court ruling described above, the government will increase the credit line in 2023 beyond the originally planned level of debt suspending debt brake by around 70 billion euros. The convergence criteria will once again not be met in 2023 and very probably also not in 2024.

Too big to fail

The state's massive interventions in the economy prevent the adjustment mechanisms of the free market economy from developing to the extent required. Companies that need to face up to tough market conditions and adapt their structures and business models are now relying on the state to bail them out.

Since the 2008 financial crisis, a large number of banks have been considered systemically relevant - "too big to fail". In order to avoid mass insolvencies and a bank run, the Financial Market Stabilisation Fund was set up in 2008 with a credit authorisation of 480 billion euros, of which 400 billion euros was for guarantees and 80 billion euros for investments. At times, up to 25 percent of the balance sheet total of the German banking industry was stabilised by measures of the Financial Market Stabilisation Fund (FMS).[43] The FMS was a necessary emergency measure in view of the global bank failures triggered by high-risk speculation by American banks in the real estate sector, which got into difficulties when the property bubble burst.

The global spread of what was initially a regional problem on the American continent shook confidence in the financial system to the core and is still having an impact today. The unwillingness of banks to lend money to each other and the restrictive approach to lending to companies also led to a brief but massive economic slump, the likes of which Germany had not seen since the Second World War. The German economy shrank by almost six percent in 2009, while the eurozone slumped by 4.5 per cent.[44] Ten years later, the shock is still deeply felt. The coronavirus pandemic once again caused the global economy to falter. German economic output fell by almost four per cent and the eurozone by 6.1 per cent. This time, almost all economies were hit. Global gross domestic product fell by 2.8 per cent in 2020. The response to this global economic crisis was once again huge government financial injections. A drift into a prolonged recession with high unemployment was to be avoided at all costs. In 2023, with the pandemic barely digested, there was another crisis.

Russia's invasion of Ukraine developed into a multi-year trench war that the aggressor had not expected and triggered an energy crisis that particularly affected Germany, which is dependent on Russian gas. Shortly afterwards, a military conflict broke out in the Middle East between Israel and the terrorist organisation Hamas in the Gaza Strip, with the potential to drag the entire region into the maelstrom.

In this mixed situation, China's economic performance to support the global economy is also no more available. The longstanding construction boom, which has been a key driver of the Chinese economy, has run out of steam. Large construction companies are on the verge of insolvency. In light of the impressions of the last decade and the enormous failures to maintain Germany's competitiveness as an industrial location and to drive forward digitalisation and the transformation to a climate-neutral economy, it is not surprising that politicians react in panic as soon as a company threatens to cut jobs due to its imbalance and calls for state aid. Jobs and full employment make a significant contribution to securing social peace.

This book has already reported on the heated atmosphere at this time in connection with migration. According to a communication from the European Commission, 170 national measures totalling 540 billion euros were approved across the EU by the end of 2022 to support companies.[45] The measures include favourable loans, grants, guarantees and state investments. Germany is in first place with a share of 49 per cent, ahead of France (30 per cent) and Italy (five per cent). According to the German Business Panel (GBP) - a German research community with more than 100 scientists - companies that had already benefited from corona aid are once again calling for state aid during the 2023 energy crisis.[46]

Large corporations in particular, with hundreds of thousands of employees, capitalise on their dominance and see themselves as systemically relevant. The entire SME sector and in particular the numerous craft businesses are falling through the cracks. The traffic light government feels compelled to give companies another helping hand. But the powder has long since been shot. The entrepreneurial risk is being shamelessly passed on to the state and thus to the general public.

The dead end

Once again, German politicians are using the nightmare image of a recession to justify the repeated suspension of the debt brake or at least an extension of it. In view of the necessary transformation of the national economy to a sustainable model, many prominent politicians and experts consider the debt rule, which was only introduced in 2010, outdated. It prevents (government) investment in the future. Following the aforementioned ruling by the Federal Constitutional Court, federal budgets see no other way out than to declare 2023 an emergency and legitimise new debt.

The accumulated mountain of debt can only be overcome by continued refinancing, i.e. by postponing the avalanche of debt into the future, tax increases and higher revenues from the growth effect of the economy. Higher taxes are not a very popular means of combating budget deficits. Politicians are therefore continuing to focus on continued economic growth. As a result, we are being asked to continue to drive up our consumption unabated. But will this really help us to escape the financial grip?

A look across the pond regularly provides us with a widely observed spectacle performed by the government of the United States of America. In May 2023, Treasury Secretary Janet Yellen turned to the Republican majority leader in the House of Representatives and informed him that the government would probably no longer be able to meet its payment obligations by 1 June of the same year. The debt ceiling, which was already reached in January 2023 at 31.5 trillion dollars, would not allow any further increase without the approval of the House of Representatives and Congress. According to the economist and former president of the US Federal Reserve, a default could trigger a global financial earthquake, cause financial markets to collapse and trigger panic worldwide.[47]

The play has been performed more than 100 times. That is how many times the debt ceiling of the US federal budget has been raised again and again since its introduction in 1917 during the First World War. This time, the members of both houses have even agreed to suspend the debt ceiling until 2025, albeit with a virtually frozen budget. This will not be the last time that the debt is increased further.

The Congressional Budget Office (CBO) is forecasting a budget deficit of USD 1.5 trillion for 2023. By 2033, according to the forecast, the deficit will have almost doubled to 2.7 trillion dollars.[48] In terms of gross domestic product (GDP), the shortfall will increase from six to 6.9 per cent in 2033 -well above the 50-year average of 3.6 per cent, as the report states. As a result, the debt level will rise from 98 per cent of GDP to 119 per cent - at USD 46.7 trillion, the highest debtlevel ever statistically recorded in the USA. There is no end in sight. For comparison: the International Monetary Fund estimates the gross national product of the European Union at17.8 trillion euros in 2023.

Getting into debt is en vogue. Everyone does it and everyone justifies it in the same way: necessary restructuring of the economy, combating a looming recession, maintaining social peace. The spending spree knows no bounds. From 1947 to 2008 (the year of the global financial crisis), the annual US budget deficit of 2.5 per cent of GDP was only twice higher. In the following 14 years it was already nine times higher.[49] The CBO's projection suggests that we will not reach the historic level again.

The next pandemic, the next far-reaching military conflict or the next natural disaster are almost certainly to be expected in the coming decades. By continuing to build up debt, governments around the world have dangerously robbed themselves of their ability to act and are leading us into a dead end that demands ever more growth.

The flood of money

Anyone who takes out a loan must find a willing lender. To cover its budget deficit, a state usually issues governmentbonds, which, depending on the state's credit rating, represent a safe and usually high-interest investment for an investor. By issuing the bonds, the state withdraws money from investors that would otherwise be spent on consumption and instead finances investments that benefit the general public. In large periods, this is a zero-sum game in terms of the available money supply. However, if the state's hunger for money is not matched by sufficient savings, the central bank comes into play. It is able to create money without the state having to provide anything in return.

The financial and subsequent euro and global economic crisis triggered by the bursting of the US real estate bubble in 2007 caused all monetary and financial policy dams to collapse. High-risk speculation by banks with derivatives that were secured by mortgage loans and bonds with the lowest credit rating – so-called Asset Backed Securities (ABS) – led some American banks[5] into insolvency. The final straw came in 2008 with the collapse of the US investment bank Lehmann Brothers in New York. Neither the British Barclays Bank, as a major investor, nor the then US Treasury Secretary Henry Paulson were prepared to provide further funds to avert the bankruptcy. The consequences of this seemingly localized event revealed the fragility of the global financial system. Banks on all continents were forced to write down their investments on a large scale and became insolvent. The financial crisis even led to state bankruptcies, Greece in 2012 and again in 2015, Ireland in 2011. Italy, Spain and Portugal were saved from insolvency by rescue packages.

The spreading wave of bank failures meant that no bank trusted any other bank - interbank trading came to a temporary standstill. The central banks of the USA, the EU and Japan intervened with massive injections of money. The European Central Bank (ECB) alone intervened with a cash injection of 335 billion euros[50] and allowed the central banks of the member states to lend freshly printed money at low interest rates almost indefinitely.[51] In order to put a stop to the death of banks and to

---

[5] Bear Stearns, Fannie Mae and Freddie Mac were the first major banks to file for bankruptcy due to the high loss in value of their structural assets, but were rescued by government aid.

help the countries in difficulty – first and foremost Greece and Ireland – and companies in the midth of the financial and economic crisis and provide them with sufficient liquidity – which the lenders had withdrawn form these countries – the governments of the European Union decided to launch one rescue package after another.[6] With the first two rescue packages in 2010 and 2011 totalling 225 billion euros, Greece's debt amounted to 111 per cent of its gross domestic product. This mainly benefited French creditors, who were invested with 112 billion euros.[52] At the same time, the European Financial Stability Facility (EFSF) with a total financing and guarantee framework of 780 billion euros and the Securities Markets Programme (SMP) with a volume of 218 billion euros were launched in March and May 2010. This was followed by the European Financial Stabilisation Mechanism (€60 billion), which was replaced in October 2012 by the European Stability Mechanism (EFSM) with a volume of €700 billion, in line with the famous saying of the then President of the European Central Bank, Mario Draghi - "Whatever it takes". Not all of the facilities were fully utilised.

In addition to these rescue packages, some central banks also used the printing press directly by means of so-called ELA loans (Emergency Liquidity Assistance). These are loans that

---

[6] A detailed description of the events during the financial and economic crisis from 2008 to 2021 can be found in Hans-Werner Sinn, "Die wunderbare Geldvermehrung", Verlag Herder 2021

national central banks are authorised to grant to banks in their own country independently and on their own terms in the event of an emergency. Greece, Ireland and Cyprus made use of this option during the financial crisis. The Belgian central bank also used ELA loans to rescue Fortis Bank, while the German Bundesbank used ELA loans to support Hypo Real Estate. Hans-Werner Sinn, a professor of economics, calculated the amount of liquidity created in this way to be EUR 251 billion by June 2021.[53]

The EU's central bank money supply, also known as the monetary base (M0), doubled from 0.89 trillion euros to 1.77 trillion euros between July 2008 (start of the financial crisis) and July 2012 as a result of the measures described above. The financial and euro crisis as well as the economic downturns in 2009 and 2012 seemed to have been overcome. The rescue packages had taken effect and foreign investors were gradually regaining confidence in the crisis-hit countries. Afterall, Mario Draghi had promised them quasi reinsurance at zero cost in the event of defaults.

Interestingly, the expansion of base money initially had hardly any impact on the real economy. The additional liquidity merely filled the gap created by the flight of capital from the crisis-ridden Mediterranean countries or disappeared into the financial sector, where speculation was already in full swing again. It had actually been expected that prices would rise due to the increase in the money supply - which was also the case between mid-2009 and the end of 2011 - but from 2012, inflation was on the decline again and reached its minimum of minus 0.6 per cent in January 2015. The response to the feared deflation and signs of a weakening economy was Mario Draghi's "the Trillion Euro Bazooka".[54]

This measure by the European Central Bank, known as the Quantitative Easing policy, comprised an extensive purchase programme of public and private sector securities, a reduction in the refinancing rate for banks (base rate) from a low of one percent to minus 0.1 percent and the issue of targeted longer-term refinancing credits (TLTROs) to banks in order to stimulate lending in the private sector.[55] Ultimately, in order to finally allow the money that has been hoarded to have an impact on the real economy and to raise inflation to the target corridor of plus/minus two percent. From October 2014 to June 2023, around 3.5 trillion euros were pumped into the market through the purchase of government securities.

The full force of the ignited bazooka became apparent at the outbreak of the coronavirus pandemic, when the world experienced the most massive economic slump since the Second World War, and culminated in a price explosion following Russia's attack on Ukraine and the resulting energy crisis, which reached 11.5 percent in October 2022. At this point, the amount of central bank money totalled over six trillion euros, more than seven times as much as before the outbreak of the financial crisis.

The consequences of this excessive monetary policy have been and continue to be felt first-hand by every citizen. The long period of low interest rates depleted the savings and retirement savings of many average earners. Many banks even demanded penalty interest on their customers' deposits from a sum of money of usually 50,000 euros. Life insurance policies, a cornerstone of retirement provision for German citizens in particular, are hardly worth the paper they are written on with a guaranteed interest rate of 0.25 per cent (since 2022). The returns are being wiped out by inflation. The immense amount of money represents a constant risk of inflation and thus devaluation of our money. In order to keep it under control, central banks are raising key interest rates, making loans more expensive..

The debt service of highly indebted countries becomes a heavy burden, as described in the previous section, and limits the ability to react to new crises. It should not go unmentioned that loose monetary policy is not a European invention.

The Japanese central bank is regarded as a pioneer of the quantitative easing policy and has been pursuing it for several decades. It goes without saying that the USA also repeatedly put together new investment packages - on credit - during the crisis years. And China, the world's second-largest economy, is also constantly keeping its economy going with monetary and fiscal policy measures. So the jug can be led to the well for a long time before it breaks.

In combination with an unbridled debt policy, we are being forced to continue focussing on economic growth. At a special meeting in Lisbon in March 2000, the EuropeanCouncil formulated "sustainable economic growth" as a prerequisite for achieving its strategic goal for the coming decade of "making the Union the most competitive and dynamic knowledge-based economy in the world".[56] This view has not changed to this day.

From the perspective of 2024, however, the signs are anything but rosy. China, the locomotive that once kept the world going with double-digit growth rates, has already slowed down massively and is joining the ranks of the only moderately growing developed economies. Global economic output is expected to shrink further in 2024 and 2025. And the geopolitical environment continues to point to increasing conflicts and persistence in crisis mode. However, mountains of debt leave little room for manoeuvre to respond adequately to these challenges. The missing funds can only be raised through further debt or higher revenues. The debt burden requires low interest rates to give it a chance of being reduced. The escalating money supply and indexed inflation in turn force the central banks to keep interest rates high. In the end, we remain prisoners of a system designed for growth, like the anchor between the magnets of an electric motor. We are the anchor - forced to consume at ever higher speeds, with all its fatal consequences for us and our planet. We are sitting on a powder keg that will explode sooner or later if we do not come to our senses and adopt a different financial and economic policy.

Trust in Innovation

We humans generally find it difficult to deal with major changes. Especially when we are supposed to drive them forward ourselves. The first locomotives, which travelled through the vastness of the country with a loud snout and steam, amazed and frightened the people of their time in equal measure. Passengers who were exposed to the regular rattling as they travelled over the rail interfaces were predicted to suffer incurable brain damage. The first rattling and still slow automobiles were not believed to have a future. But despite all the reservations, the idea of motorized vehicles could not be stopped.

Innovations still scare us today. All the more so, the less we are able to understand the invention itself and assess its consequences. In this respect, we in the 21st century hardly differ from our ancestors in the pre-industrial age. On the other hand, it is all the more astonishing that the majority of people are firmly convinced that innovations will solve the problems of the future. A trust in God has become naturalised, along the lines of "somehow it will work out". In the fight against the "unavoidable consequences of climate change", former German Education and Research Minister Anja Karliczek placed her trust in "the innovative power of German science and industry.[57]

Artificial Intelligence

Great hope is pinned on the breakthrough of artificial intelligence, or AI for short. Since the publication of a free version of ChatGPT by the company OpenAI, the topic of computer-aided intelligence has become part of everyday life. You can ask ChatGPT anything and receive almost print-ready presentations on any topic you choose. Even online editorial teams are already relying on ChatGPT in some cases. It works incredibly fast. ChatGPT produces answers to complex questions in a matter of seconds, which would have taken us days with conventional research.

Artificial intelligence helps us to draw up a budget, conduct negotiations, write a letter of condolence or explain why popcorn "pops".[58] The significance of GPT and the numerous competing products such as Neuroflash, Copy.ai, TensorFlow from Google or Grok from Elon Musk and the sometimes amusing use of its "intelligence" lies in the revolutionary processes and algorithms of the software. Neural networks and the mass processing of data to train the AI system enable the programme to compose pieces of music of various genres, generate images from texts and create interpretations and summaries of books as if they had sprung from a human brain.

The analytical capabilities and speed of these systems make it possible, for example, to efficiently control the complex material flows and production steps in a factory and reduce the consumption of materials, auxiliary and operating supplies and the use of energy. Chatbots, fed with comprehensive operating and product information, conduct customer conversations in the same way as their flesh-and blood colleagues, who they are increasingly replacing in service. In China, avatars moderate entire knowledge programmes on television. AI is already present in many applications and will completely change our everyday lives. Humanoid robots will work day and night without getting tired and ease the acute shortage of skilled labour, especially in Germany, in the coming years. AI combined with super and quantum computers will enable the discovery of new materials in just a few years due to their rapid speed and bring them to production maturity. Research and development will experience exponential new heights and breakthroughs and radically change our lives.

"At some point, you will simply tell the computer what you want and it will do all these tasks for you," said company founder Sam Altman in his opening speech at OpenAI's first developer conference in November 2023. New functions allow every user to create their own AI assistant – without any programming knowledge. This means that anyone can become a developer in the open-source universe. The potential is huge.

Artificial intelligence is not the only innovation of our age. However, it is a very effective catalyst for the development of new processes and products as well as basic research. Robotics and AI methods of image recognition are already being used in organ transplants today and perform them more precisely than an overtired surgeon can after ten hours of work. It is conceivable that in a few years' time, the replacement of organs could take place as smoothly as the assembly line production of a car. Chief and senior physicians will only monitor the procedure in the event of an unforeseen emergency, like the driver of an autonomous train.

Limits of the progress

The author is also convinced that technological progress will revolutionise our lives at ever shorter intervals. In publications on this topic, the term disruptive technologies is used in an inflationary way. The changes take place in quantum leaps – not in a linear glide - that pull us into a maelstrom that makes us feel dizzy, and we will have less and less time to find our way in the new world.

The microcosm in which we live and know our way around, on which our truths and insights are based, is being significantly unbalanced. Our previous world view and familiar environment are being erased, which is why the change has a disruptive effect. The question is: "Will these massive upheavals bring about the resolution of the challenges we are facing?" What impact will digitalisation, artificialintelligence and robotics have on sustainable business? Will advances in quantum technology eliminate the shortage of resources on earth? As highlighted in the previous chapters, the topic of well-being is also primarily about wellbeing. So how will these leaps in development affect social coexistence?

The research group "Digitalisation for Sustainability – Science in Dialogue" (D4S), led by Prof. Dr. Tilman Santarius, TU Berlin, is at least critical of current developments and calls for a reorientation of policy in the area of digitalisation.[59] The main argument: most government initiatives fail to take into account the far-reaching consequences of digitalisation in terms of the environment, sustainability and social peace.

This book has already referred to the hunger for energy of digital devices, data centres and digital applications. The scientist and founder of the Digiconomist research institute has estimated the global electricity demand for the use of artificial intelligence based on the forecast sales of AI chips – dominated by Nvidia - at 85 to 134 terawatt hours (TWh), or in other words 85 to 134 billion kilowatt hours (kWh), of electricity per year by 2027.[60] This would correspond to the annual demand of the Netherlands. In 2022, AI in the EU accounted for around 25 percent of the calculated electricity consumption for digital infrastructure (data centres plus telecommunications services) of 70 to 95 terawatt hours (TWh). This corresponds to 2.8 to 3.8 percent of the European Union's total electricity demand.[61] However, the extent varies greatly in the individual member states and ranges from just 2.2 percent of national electricity demand in France to the IT heavyweight Ireland with 18 percent, depending on the level of development of the infrastructure and the number and size of the data centres located there. A report by the Office of Technology Assessment of the German Bundestag from October 2022 predicts a tripling of electricity consumption for information and communication technology by 2030 if not all opportunities to increase the energy efficiency of the components used are utilised. According to the report, "ICT energy consumption is already on an economically significant scale". This includes end devices, which are not included in the aforementioned statistics. In the best-case scenario, the authors believe that the hunger for energy could also decrease.[62] A Bitkom study from 2023, on the other hand, is much more sceptical and states: "Although the efficiency of IT provision has increased by 500 percent since 2010, energy requirements are continuously increasing".[63] Another problem that is a burden on the environment is air conditioning and cooling. The authors Pengfei Li, Jianyi Yang, Mohammad A. Islam, Shaolei Ren estimate the global water requirement for temperature control of the aggregates from AI applications alone at 4.2 to 6.6 trillion cubic metres in 2027. This would be equivalent to the annual water consumption of Denmark or half the water consumption of the UK.[64]

Permanently available energy is an indispensable prerequisite for the world we live in today and our well-being. Almost everyone has experienced the consequences of a power cut lasting just a few hours. The world, both big and small, suddenly comes to a standstill. Rien ne va plus - nothing works any more.

It's good if the diesel emergency generator has been regularly serviced and can step in in this case. Technology itself has made us highly dependent on it. Anyone who grows up with smartphones and the internet today hardly knows the analogue basis on which these systems were once developed. It is difficult to imagine our future without electricity. The development of renewable energy sources and their equally sustainable production is therefore a fundamental prerequisite for lasting prosperity on this planet.

In addition to our dependence on information and communication technology, our economic, social, working and private lives have become considerably more vulnerable and susceptible to attack. We experience cyberattacks on authorities, institutions and companies on an almost daily basis. Quantum computers will make today's encryption methods obsolete in just a few years. Quantum computing, i.e. computing with Qbits, is already being used today on conventional computers by means of simulation. System failures triggered by natural disasters, military conflicts and criminal activities are likely to occur more frequently in the future. Our socio-economic system has become considerably more vulnerable.

The 15 experts from eight nations involved in the D4Sproject mentioned above criticise the fact that current efforts in the areas of digital applications and artificial intelligence are mainly subordinated to the primacy of growth and the optimisation of existing structures and processes. The recognisable trend is leading to a manifestation of the status quo of a growth- and consumption-driven society. Neither the European "Green Deal" nor the EU's "Fit for the Digital Age" programme address the possibilities of shaping a sustainable future and the risks associated with digital technologies. The main aim of the programmes is to establish and secure the competitiveness of European companies. However, if economic growth is the overriding goal of this policy, it is likely to run counter to the necessary transformations towards greater sustainability, biodiversity, waste avoidance, limiting global warming and reducing environmental pollution, according to the scientists.

Today, digital market power lies with just a few companies. On the stock market, the US giants Alphabet, Amazon, Apple, Meta, Microsoft, Nvidia and Tesla are already known as the "Magnificent Seven". At almost eleven trillion euros, their market capitalisation is five times higher than all German stock corporations listed on the DAX, MDax and TechDax.[65] Their influence on the design of digital applications and structures is correspondingly high. In China, Alibaba, Tencent and Pinduoduo have captivated hundreds of millions of users and created a consumer addiction. The TikTok app from Beijing-based company Byte Dance alone has now been downloaded 1.2 billion times. More than 800 million users gather on all of the internet giant's platforms every day. According to a survey by Blog2Social, 4.8 billion people actively used social media platforms in 2023.[66] That corresponds to more than half of the world's population. The oligopolists have one thing in common: the pursuit of profit maximization. This is achieved by having users - a suggestive description for consumers - use the paid offers and products for as long and as often as possible or buy them. Temu, a sales platform from the Chinese internet company Pinduoduo, is currently taking households around the world by storm with its sophisticated, manipulative product advertising based on artificial intelligence, and has become the best in class.

Pinduoduo invests huge sums in marketing this blockbuster. Not a trace of restraint, sustainability or public welfare. The Chinese government felt compelled to force the founder and Chief Executive Officer of the Alibaba conglomerate, Jack Ma, to resign and demand the break-up of the company, which dominates all areas of society. The dominant market position of the internet giant founded by a former teacher and the accumulated wealth of its owners mutated into a threat to the authoritarian regime.

If we look at the data collected by the International Resource Panel[7] another disappointing trend becomes apparent: the unstoppable increase in global material consumption. Despite or, as mentioned in the previous section, precisely because of technological progress, the global use of raw materials has in-

---

[7] The International Resource Panel (IRP) was established in 2007 by the United Nations Environment Programme (UNEP) to build and share the knowledge needed to improve the use of our resources worldwide.

creased by more than 20 percent in the last eleven years from 2010 to 2021. Since the collection of data from 200 countries worldwide in 1970, the use of materials by countries has increased continuously despite rapid technological progress. At the same time, the material intensity required to generate one US dollar of national economic output has fallen sharply. In 1970, 1.157kilograms of material were needed to generate one US dollar of domestic product in the USA. In 2021, it was only 0.372kilograms. In the same period, however, total material consumption increased 1.3-fold. In Europe, the measured material intensity fell from one to half a kilogramme per one US dollar of national product.[67] Material consumption rose by 40 per cent in the same period. Globally, material use even increased 3.2-fold between 1970 and 2021. This is mainly due to China, which accounts for around a third of total material consumption.

In the coming years, a further increase in the consumption of raw materials in the high single-digit percentage range can be expected, even in the developed economic zones. The figures confirm earlier studies on the impact of progress on material efficiency. The acclaimed digital progress does not appear to provide us with the necessary effect of a balanced eco-balance. In his analysis of the state of the scientific post-growth debate, Dirk Posse states: "There is a consensus among growth critics that it is not possible to decouple environmental consumption and economic growth and that technical solutions are not sufficient."[68]

If the development path we have chosen does not help us in our endeavours to operate in regenerative cycles, we can still expect that at least the prosperity of all of us will continue to improve or, at worst, be maintained, and that poverty and hunger - the eradication of which are the first two of the United Nations' 17 sustainability goals - will be a thing of the past worldwide. The scientists of the D4S project do not give us much hope in this aspect either. Under the given parameters, their stakeholders and political leaders, inequality, concentration of power and polarisation between the beneficiaries of modern technologies and those at whose expense these benefits are achieved will tend to increase.

Income and opportunity inequality will most likely increase. The researchers justify this with the increasing qualification requirements in the production sector, which are correspondingly better paid, and the significantly lower requirements in the service sector, which are therefore paid less. Another driver of inequality is capital income.[69] Those who are rich get richer. Those who are poor remain so.

Urbanisation and living in tenements have led to more people living together in smaller spaces. More than half of the world's population lives in cities. And yet these multi-generational places have tended to divide us rather than bring us together in our social behaviour. Both the Western world, which is characterised by a market economy, and Eastern socialism have promoted self-centred behaviour and have allowed thinking about the common good to fall by the wayside. The consumer prosperity of the individual has become more important than the well-being of the community.

Talking to a humanoid robot may be more entertaining than talking to an overtired human carer who is rushing from one appointment to the next. However, the lack of contact with other people reinforces the effect of isolation and emerging loneliness. Only interpersonal relationships enable the social community to develop further. The Covid pandemic has impressively demonstrated the consequences of the lack of interpersonal encounters. Video calls and conferences can bridge such a phase, but cannot permanently replace direct personal contact. The challenges we face require strong cohesion and consensus among international communities.

Technological progress will make our everyday lives easier in many ways, relieve us of tedious routine tasks and increase the chances of curing even previously untreatable diseases. There are numerous promising approaches in research and development that could make our lives more sustainable in the long term. Supercritical water at a depth of ten kilometres under the earth's crust could solve the energy problem. There is already a pilot power plant in Iceland. Vertical farming could significantly reduce the amount of agricultural land required and help to end hunger. However, all these activities do not automatically lead to an ecosystem within the boundaries of our planet. Whether or not these technologies have a positive effect on our coexistence and therefore generate lasting prosperity depends on whether we can give the research and development efforts a lasting "Purpose" or adhere to the laws of the growth spiral.

Capitalism versus Socialism

In discussions and publications on the subject of climate change, it is often argued that it is capitalism that is damaging our planet. So should we turn to socialism? Will we find the salutary solution in a socialist form of society? Are people more environmentally aware under socialism? Does the economy use resources in a more environmentally friendly way under socialism? These questions can be answered with a clear "no". Whether we look at Cuba, Russia or the former GDR, even in these communist or socialist-led countries, considerable overexploitation of natural resources and the ecosystem has been and continues to be practised. The desire for consumption is no less. This can be seen very clearly in the example of China. The country has achieved rapid growth like no other before it - comparable to the reconstruction of Germany after the Second World War - over the last 40 years and has raised the prosperity of its population to an upper middle level (as defined by the World Bank). Adjusted per capita net income has multiplied by a factor of 57 from USD148 to USD 8,394 between 1979 and 2019.[70] In the same period, Germany's adjusted per capita net income only quadrupled, while that of the USA increased sixfold. Nevertheless, Germany's per capita income is still 4.6 times higher and the USA's 6.6 times higher than in the Middle Kingdom. China is now one of the largest consumer markets in the world in many areas. However, the enormous economic growth has come at a high price. The People's Republic is held responsible for 30 per cent of global greenhouse gas emissions - as of 2021. Measured in terms of economic output, CO2 emissions per 1 US dollar are three times higher than in the eurozone and twice as high as in the United States. Almost 100 percent of the population is exposed to particulate matter pollution of more than ten micrograms per cubic metre (for comparison: Germany 89 percent; EU 80 percent; USA 3.3 percent).[71] A value of more than ten micrograms per cubic meter is classified as harmful to health according to the guidelines of the World Health Organization (WHO). Emissions of methane gas, which is considered to be the even more aggressive greenhouse gas, were three times higher in China in 2018 than in the EU (excluding Great Britain) and twice as high as the methane pollution from the USA.

Radical deforestation in the Middle Kingdom already led to a lowering of the groundwater table in many provinces at the end of the 1990s and is increasingly jeopardising the drinking water supply in China. The hunger for raw materials and consumer goods in the emerging, communist-led second largest economic power in the world is enormous. Manufacturers of luxury goods, from wristwatches to premium cars, find their biggest sales markets there. There is a lot of catching up to do. Environmental awareness, on the other hand, is still very low.

It remains to be said: Neither capitalism nor socialism or communism differ in terms of their impact on environmental pollution, greenhouse gas emissions and stress on the ecosystem. Even the forces of a free market obviously do not lead to an equalisation of the supply of planetary goods and their demand by the constantly growing population of the earth. The old-fashioned competition between systems therefore leads to a dead end. It is necessary to raise our society and our economic system to a new level. We must make the quantum leap to progress as the Norwegian economic philosopher Anders Indset describes in his book "Quantum Economy".[72] However, it is not enough for individual societies to renew themselves in isolation. A global regulatory corrective is needed to promote the necessary changes. There is only one planet Earth, on which we all depend together. The climate knows no borders and no ideological differences.

In its October 2021 report, the International Monetary Fund (IMF) states: "Achieving the reductions in green- house gas emissions needed to mitigate global warming will require a transformation of the global economy."[73] Diese Transformation bedingt den Wandel von intensiv CO2-emittierenden Prozessen und umweltbelastenden Arbeitsplätzen hin zu nachhaltigen Tätigkeiten, die zu einer Verringerung der Erderwärmung beitragen und zu einem ausgewogeneren Ökosystem führen. In einem solchen Wirtschaftsmodell wird Dienstleistung eine zentrale Rolle spielen. Eine dienstleistungsorientierte Gesellschaft dürfte auch zu deutlich höherer Zufriedenheit mit der Arbeit führen, als es in einem überwiegend materiell ausgerichteten, auf höchste Produktivität angelegten Wirtschaftssystem möglich erscheint. Diese Annahme begründet sich in Studien zu den beeinflussenden Faktoren der Lebenszufriedenheit. This transformation requires a shift from intensive CO_2-emitting processes and environmentally harmful jobs to sustainable activities that contribute to a reduction in global warming and lead to a more balanced ecosystem. Services will play a central role in such an economic model. A service-orientated society is also likely to lead to significantly higher satisfaction with work than would appear possible in a predominantly material-oriented economic system geared towards maximum productivity. This assumption is based on studies on the factors influencing life satisfaction. The higher the income of a population group and the more basic needs such as food, housing and work are met, the more factors such as social recognition, appreciation, leisure activities, personal development opportunities and meaningful activities become important. Wealth is not the most important thing: we are happiest in strong, trusting relationships.[74] According to the United Nations World Happiness Report 2023, people in Germany, which is one of the richest countries in the world, seem to become increasingly unhappy. Above a certain income level, which Nobel Prize-winning economists Daniel Kahneman and Angus Deaton put at 75,000 US dollars a year in their study, life satisfaction hardly increases at all. Finland is one of the countries where the population feels happiest. Researcher and HR marketing expert Helena Schneider attributes this result to the promotion of interpersonal relationships in the Scandinavian country. "People are encouraged to build and maintain strong, healthy relationships with their families, friends and the community."[75]

The future-proof company

Companies are facing extraordinary challenges today. The change in climate policy calls for CO_2-neutral manufacturing processes and sustainable products. The rapid development in the field of digitalisation and artificial intelligence is calling many business models into question. The globally esteemed "Made in Germany" label, based on excellent engineering and high-quality machines, is becoming a minor matter. Instead of sophisticated, robust hardware, the controlling software and its intelligent scope of performance are becoming the decisive quality feature. While the traditional car industry is still focussed on catching up with the development of the so-called NEV, New Electric Vehicle, software companies are already testing the means of transport of the day after tomorrow. The decisive factor will no longer be the number of cylinders and the horsepower of a car, but how comfortably and entertainingly we get from A to B. Autonomous vehicles will whizz us to our destination without any hectic rush or traffic jams, while passengers entertain their children, quickly prepare an important presentation or relax at a conference. However, the more the "transport" service takes centre stage, the less important the car becomes as a status symbol. Assuming progressive mobility concepts and sustainable urban planning, the demand for cars in private households will decrease significantly or even disappear completely.

The need for climate-neutral manufacturing processes and changing lifestyles will cause numerous industries to disappear. The economy as a whole is in a tremendous upheaval. Even if it is still too slow, there is an increasing demand for sustainable products and services.

Agility and adaptability

The survival of a company depends largely on how quickly it can adapt to changes in the markets in which it operates. The old economy is vehemently refusing to accept the new parameters of the future economy. Sometimes someone has to stand up and take the initiative against the mainstream. Elon Musk is the type of entrepreneur who takes inspiration from the unfeasible and reinvents the feasible. The genius with his eratic personality has rocked the car industry and, above all, woken German manufacturers from their hibernation. The pillar of German prosperity is beginning to totter. Amazon with Jeff Bezos, Apple with Steve Jobs, Alphabet with Larry Page, as well as Jack Ma, founder of Alibaba, and Tencent, founded by the Chinese visionary Ma Huateng (also known as Pony Ma), the Chinese counterparts, are constantly shaking up the markets with new technologies and business ideas. Uber and Didi are convincing with innovative mobility concepts and are challenging the traditional taxi guild. Creativity does not stop at the planetary atmosphere either. For Captain Kirk, the popular commander in the 1960s science fiction series "Enterprise", fiction became reality during his lifetime when actor William Shatner actually flew into space at the age of 90 in the New Shepard of Blue Origin (company of Amazon founder Jeff Bezos). Today, we routinely communicate with friends and colleagues via a smartwatch. In the 1960s, this was still fantasy. The visionaries Jeff Bezos, Richard Branson (Virgin Galactic) and Elon Musk (SpaceX) have created a completely new business model with the commercialisation of space travel.

Many traditional German companies rely all too much on the fact that they have already survived numerous crises over the past 100 years. It is to be hoped that these companies will not only weather the stormy times, but also develop strategies that will make them fit for the future. Grundig, Telefunken, Nokia, Siemens Communication or BlackBerry, once founded as Research in Motion - they all underestimated the change in market and customer behaviour because they were unable to break out of their established patterns of thinking. Back then, it was Apple that shook up the mobile phone market with its innovative iPhone.

Innovation is an indispensable driver of technical progress. However, creativity, agility and courage must be added in order to develop a successful business concept from an idea or vision. Start-ups are regarded as the modern role models. Their founders fascinate with their unshakeable conviction in their business idea. The company structures are flat, decisions are made and implemented quickly. They respond to problems by adapting. As they are convinced of their idea, their vision, the question is not whether it *can* be realised, but only *how*. This makes them resilient.[76] "Big is great" was yesterday, "small is beautiful" is the new promise. The spin-off of parts of the company, such as at Siemens or General Electric, was not only due to the realisation that hidden company values could be leveraged, but also to the understanding that the business units released into independence could act faster and more successfully on their markets independently of the parent company. The success of start-ups has prompted some companies to set up small, independent companies themselves. In these agile biotopes, creativity and inventiveness are to find their breeding ground and bring new ideas to product maturity, which are often difficult to realise in existing corporate structures.

The legendary American hedge fund manager and philanthropist Paul Tudor Jones is said to have told his traders and fellow investors to "Adapt, evolve, compete or die". Adapting to changing markets and situations, continuing to develop and accepting the competition or the challenge determines the success of the trader and likewise of the entrepreneur. Those who fail to do so will disappear from the scene. Sometimes an unexpected situation requires a lightning-fast rethink and adaptation to the new circumstances. For example, the first German commander of the International Space Station ISS, Alexander Gerst, told company managers how he was put to such a test. Expedition 57 began on 4 October 2018 with the return flight of the crew from Expedition 56. On 11 October, two more astronauts were to join their three colleagues on Expedition 57. However, the second stage of the launch vehicle failed during the approach; Soyuz MS-10 was unable to reach orbit and had to make an emergency landing. The moment the ground station announced the cancellation of the flight, the ISS commander realised that the mission would take months and it was impossible to predict when his team would be able to return to Earth. Die Crew musste sich entscheiden, die Mission und die damit verbundenen Experimente zu Dritt fortzuführen oder die ISS zu verlassen. The crew had to decide whether to continue the mission and the associated experiments with only three crew members or leave the ISS. Even before the management on the ground asked the momentous question, the members of Expedition 57 had decided in favour of a stay and began to prepare for the new situation. On 3 December 2018, Soyuz MS-11 brought three more space scientists to the ISS. Expedition 57 was successfully completed with the return of Commander Gerst and his two colleagues on 20 December 2018. It is important for a company to be able to switch quickly to the new framework conditions in a crisis and not remain in its usual operating procedures for long. This requires courageous leadership and an organisation that has learned to deal with dynamic markets.

Correctly assessing the influence of a new technology, a new invention or a new zeitgeist requires the utmost attention and structures in order to implement these findings quickly ahead of all competitors and thereby achieve a competitive edge in the market.

Traditional companies spoilt by success generally find it difficult to anticipate the shifts in their markets and to moderate the necessary adjustment process. Well-known entrepreneurs from the post-war period provide ample examples. Neckermann would rub his eyes at how Jeff Bezos revolutionised the catalogue business with Amazon and forged a globally dominant group from a book mail order company. However, the growth in size may also be to the detriment of the online retail star in the long term. In the meantime, numerous newcomers have successfully copied the digitalisation of the retail business. The internet-based platform concept still offers countless application possibilities. Constantly questioning one's own business model, organisation, production and product design is a permanent task for management in order to ensure the continued existence of the company.

Sustainability is not a strategy

Many European companies are groaning under the multitude of regulations from the European Commission in Brussels. Through their lobby organisations, the affected industries are trying to soften the requirements for sustainable business and climate protection. Mandatory sustainability reports are perceived as an imposition. The supply chain act (EU Corporate Sustainability Due Diligence Directive) being discussed in the

EU is seen as another brake on competition and a bureaucratic monster. In reality, the EU Supply Chain Act is intended to help improve working conditions worldwide, comply with labour laws and better protect human rights and the environment. In Germany, large companies (with 3,000 employees or more, or 1,000 employees from 2024) have been obliged since 2023 to regularly check their direct suppliers for violations of human rights and labour law as well as their compliance with environmental protection regulations. The duty of care covers the company's own business area, direct suppliers and indirect suppliers in Germany and abroad.[77] The law requires, among other things, the establishment of risk management, regular risk analyses, integration into the procurement process and the taking of corrective measures if units in the company's own business area or direct and indirect suppliers do not comply with legal requirements in the areas of environmental protection and human rights. Non-compliance with the provisions of the German Supply Chain Sustainability Act (LkSG)[8] can be punished with fines of up to 8,000 euros or, in the case of companies with sales of more than 400 million euros, two per cent of the global average annual sales.

These obligations are not entirely new. Similar requirement have long been part of the self-image of a well-managed company in terms of corporate governance. Adherence to applicable

---

[8] LkSG = Lieferkettensorgfaltsgesetz

laws and regulations wherever a company is active is part of the catalogue of compliance guidelines. As early as the beginning of the 2000s, Siemens and other companies were already forcing their suppliers to agree to unannounced audits to check labour relations and other possible violations of the law. The author himself has negotiated such contracts with hundreds of suppliers in China. There is no doubt that assessing the risks of vulnerable processes and operating units should be part of every company's risk management. The EU proposal goes beyond national regulations in some respects and already applies to companies with 500 employees. It also provides for the right of affected parties to sue for damages from the companies involved. As German companies are already subject to the duty of care with regard to their supply chain, the standardised obligation of all EU companies could even provide a competitive advantage.

However, a study conducted by the German Association of Materials Management, Purchasing and Logistics (BME) and the risk management company Integrity Next in 2023 revealed that only 13 per cent of the companies surveyed with more than 1,000 employees were aware of possible human rights and environmental protection violations by their direct business partners.[78] Yet incidents in this regard can have massive consequences for a company. A series of suicides at the Taiwanese electronics manufacturer Foxconn, one of the suppliers for the iPhone, due to excessively harsh working conditions put Apple under intense pressure in 2010 and exposed the tech star to international criticism. Suddenly, the trendy iPhone was stained with blood. Apple reacted and urged the world market leader in computer components to improve labour conditions immediately. The workers' wages were increased in stages by up to 70 per cent. On 24 April 2013, more than 1,000 people died in a textile factory in Bangladesh and over 2,000 others, mostly female workers, were injured. Cracks in the building walls are said to have signalled the risk of collapse days earlier. Nevertheless, the management apparently did not take any protective measures and forced the employees to continue production. An article published by the German Federal Agency for Civic Education in April 2018 stated: "Although there were numerous improvements in working conditions after the tragic event in Rana, Bangladesh, the intense competition in the textile and sporting goods industry is preventing a global improvement in working conditions in the world's sewing factories."[79] The clients of the factory in Rana included well-known European fashion companies such as Primark, Benetton, Mango, C&A, KiK and Adler and their suppliers. Under pressure from the public, a compensation fund was set up that raised more than 30 million dollars. In May 2020, an article in *Spiegel* magazine drew attention to the inhumane working conditions in cobalt mines.[80] Cobalt is mainly used in the production of lithium-ion batteries. However, the chemical element is also used in tools, medical technology, automotive construction and as a catalyst. Italian photographer Luca Catalano Gonzaga has documented the working conditions in the mines in the south of the Democratic Republic of the Congo, where children also work. 60 per cent of the world's cobalt production comes from the Congo. Zambia takes second place. In early 2024 Journalists from the ZDF television programme Frontal and Der Spiegel uncovered active involvement of employees of a BASF joint venture in the Chinese province of Xinjiang in surveillance measures of the Uyghur ethnic minority on behalf of the Chinese government. Under pressure from the Inter Parliamentary Alliance on China (IPAC), an international group of parliamentarians, BASF's CEO announced the planned sale of the joint venture shares at the beginning of February 2024. Despite repeated reports of human rights violations and alleged forced labour by Uyghurs at its plant in Xinjiang province, car manufacturer Volkswagen is sticking to its investment. The People's Republic of China is VW's largest single market, accounting for almost 40 per cent of vehicle sales. However, the pressure on VW to reduce its activities in the controversial region is increasing. BASF's example is also having an impact on other international companies. An investment that is costing companies dearly.

The comprehensive awareness of responsibility for environmentally friendly and human rights-respecting behaviour can probably not be left to the free forces of the market alone. The study cited above revealed that the majority of the companies surveyed do not take environmental and human rights aspects into account in their business decisions out of their own conviction, but only because they are forced to do so by law. As a result, companies feel compelled to set up new departments in order to fulfil the requirements of the authorities. Only a few market players see the orientation of the economy towards an ecologically balanced system as an opportunity to make their business future-proof. Anyone who wants to survive for the next 100 years should realise that this is not possible without adapting to the limits of the earth system. A few trees in the rainforest as compensation for environmentally harmful manufacturing processes is not enough. Neither is the CO_2 emissions trading scheme, which is intended to cancel out environmental offences. Sustainability starts with the initial idea for a new product. Which materials can I use without harming the environment and further reducing the available raw materials? How can the manufacturing process be designed without contributing to global warming? Can the new product be broken down into its components and reused with minimal energy input? What about the longevity of the product? Can the proportion of recycled input materials be increased?

The German Tesa company was very early on concerned about the reuse and multiple use of its products. The well-known transparent Tesa tape is now made from 90 per cent recycled PET bottles. The adhesives developed are easily detachable so that smartphone components can be removed and reused without destroying them. Tesa has set itself the goal of increasing the proportion of recycled or bio-based materials in its products to 70 per cent by 2030. Anyone who prioritises sustainability and the circular economy like Tesa must also involve their suppliers. With its corporate philosophy, Tesa is one of the German global market leaders.

Artificial intelligence, augmented reality, blockchain technology, the Internet of Things and quantum technology are the breeding ground for new products, services and innovative business models that are causing traditional industries, companies and jobs to disappear. Many companies are facing these developments completely unprepared. What's more, the new technologies are not only hitting company managers at breathtaking speed, but are also very complex and incomprehensible. In many cases, companies lack employees with the necessary expertise and know-how to develop new applications and products based on the new technologies. In addition to the speed with which these developments are progressing and are perceived as disruptive, it is important to capture the zeitgeist of sustainability and incorporate it into corporate development.

The consideration of environmental and sustainability aspects in all activities from product development to procurement, production, sales and the life cycle should become part of a company's DNA. Sustainability is not an issue that should be left to the strategy department. Sustainable thinking and action must become part of the corporate culture and be practised in all areas of the company. If sustainability becomes a matter of course for corporate management, there is no need for separate departments.

Entrepreneurship as a service

Let us dare to do a thought experiment and put the economy back to its origins. In other words, back to zero, when everyone produced everything themselves to provide for their family. People very quickly realised that their neighbour had a better talent for baking bread or hoofing horses. The service society based on the division of labour was born. Imagine if the baker next door only made baked goods in order to make his talent available to society as a service. Similarly, the architect would design houses because he is better at it than others and makes his skills available to society. This concept of mutual service was trialled by a number of municipalities in the 1960s and 1980s. One prominent example is the "global village" project initiated by the French woman Mira Al Fassa. Located on the south-east coast in the Indian state of Tamil Nadu, Auroville, also known as the "global village", was founded in the 1960s and is still home to around 2,000 inhabitants today. The idea of the French woman travelling through India was to create a place where all nations could live together peacefully and in-harmony with nature and consider the protection of the environment to be a common goal. The living laboratory experiment, as Johanna Treblin describes it in an article[81], was also supported by UNESCO in 1996. Founded on red sand, one of India's largest reforestation projects was started by the first inhabitants of modern Babylon. Today, around two million trees provide the inhabitants with shade and a pleasant climate. Auroville has remained an experiment to this day, albeit unique among the thousands of other ecovillages that have sprung up around the world. However, it can serve as a blueprint for how coexistence and the cities of the future can be organised. A central element of the community of the future is the local supply of its members, as far as possible. Food and other everyday necessities will come from the local region, and energy will be generated in a decentralised manner by the residents. The fulfilment of demand for goods follows the idea of service and not profit maximisation. Money will certainly only exist digitally in the form of cryptocurrencies and will once again serve the original purpose of simplifying the exchange of goods and services. Speculation is alien to this economic model. Speculation makes no contribution to the gross prosperity product. Prosperity is no longer expressed in material wealth, but in the degree to which the community is provided for and finds fulfilment in its contribution to the society. This vision has remained a utopia in Auroville to this day and will perhaps never be realised in this form. However, it is crucial that we embark on a process of transformation that brings us closer into harmony with nature and our ecosystem. And to question whether the accumulation of material goods brings the desired sense of well-being and the certainty that we will still be sitting at a set table tomorrow and will not have to worry about our provisions and will be in a community that will be there for us when we need it. Technological progress will make it happen that we will hardly have to do anything ourselves to produce goods. Even complicated organ transplants are already being carried out more reliably by machines than by the most experienced surgeons, who are increasingly overtired demonstrating their skills at the operating table. Nobody has to do monotonous work on an assembly line any more. Intelligent robots will be able to carry out such tasks much more productively and at any time of day or night. Some products could even be manufactured and delivered on demand at the touch of a button. We can therefore allocate resources much more economically and use them when we need them. Stockpiling production would be completely absurd.

The freed-up working time will be available for more intellectual, artistic and other socially relevant tasks. Care for the elderly and social care will be much more important than they are today. The use of surplus non-working time (as we understand 'working' today) and its meaningful utilisation is probably one of the greatest challenges of the future. One could argue that we have managed to do this several times in the past. Despite the continuous reduction in working hours over more than 100 years since industrialisation, we will still reach full employment in 2023. On the contrary, there is a shortage of urgently needed skilled labour in Europe's industrialised countries, with the number of apprenticeships on offer far exceeding demand. In Germany in particular, this development can be traced back to a misguided and backward looking industrial and education policy. Not only are there too few craftsmen and employees in the service sectors, there is also a lack of sufficient teachers to guarantee a high level of training to meet the requirements of the future. According to the President of the German Teachers' Association, Heinz-Peter Meidinger, the number of unfilled teaching positions in Germany in 2023 was between 32,000 and 40,000. Many hours of the planned curricula had to be cancelled.[82] The situation may worsen considerably in the future due to the inadequate training of teachers. The politicians' response to the shortage of specialists and teachers appears to be more actionist than following a long-term, forward-looking concept.

Numerous companies claim that the customer is at the centre of their activities. But is that true? The tough targets set for employees speak a different language. Investors also expect the highest possible return on their investment and not the company's maximum contribution to society. The service concept we are talking about here first poses the question: What benefit does my product, my offer have for the buyer? As Tim Jackson puts it: "Rather, we should interpret the company's goal as providing "human services" that improve the quality of life…".[83] This business model is not about maximising material throughput, but about focussing on customer benefit. In addition to the immediate demand for food, clothing, shelter and medical care, this also includes maintaining an ecological balance and protecting our livelihoods. The benefits of food lie primarily in providing people with sufficient energy and vital substances to maintain their health. The excessive consumption of mostly unhealthy sweets and other foods, on the other hand, leads to a deterioration in physical constitution with the well-known symptoms of diabetes, high blood pressure, obesity and other metabolic disorders. Full medical practices and studies show that a growing number of people are consuming more food and sweets than a healthy diet requires. According to Statista, almost three billion people are overweight. The cost to the community could more than double over the next decade from two billion US dollars today.[84] The prevalence of diabetes 2 is growing particularly rapidly in low- and middle-income countries. The global direct healthcare costs for the treatment of diabetes already amount to almost a trillion dollars, and the trend is rising.[85] Those who are serious about customer benefit tend to sort the sweets into less exposed storage locations.

The service orientation in this post-growth approach is not limited to the expansion of the conventional service industry, which also relies in part on a high material throughput, but refers to the orientation of economic activities towards the purpose that the customer wants to achieve with them. The product plays a subordinate role and is only the vehicle for realising the benefit. When it comes to the topic transportation, which has already been mentioned, it's more about how I can get from A to B in the most comfortable way. We are therefore concentrating our efforts on the best possible means of transport and optimal transport routes with the least negative impact on our environment and climate. If we think consistently, there will be less and less private transport by car. Some German city planners are deliberately reducing the number of parking spaces in new development areas in order to encourage residents to use public transport, car-sharing models and other innovative mobility options. Car manufacturers and the supplier industry are undergoing a radical transformation.

If we place people and nature - synonymous with the surrounding ecosystem - at the centre of economic activity, we arrive at completely different corporate guidelines. The company sees itself as a social entity, embedded in the community, which on the one hand provides work as social participation, and on the other hand provides the needs of the social community to achieve and maintain an appropriate level of prosperity. Founding fathers such as Werner-von-Siemens invested in company-owned sports facilities and libraries. They contributed to keeping employees healthy in their own recreational facilities until these costly social contributions fell victim to shareholder value and economic value added approach as a measure of business value contribution. In Germany, comparable social commitment and the understanding of being an integral element of the social fabric can still be found above all in family and owner-managed companies. This is where a transformation towards a service-oriented corporation should be most likely to be realised. The question is justified as to whether, under the new parameters it makes economic sense and is necessary to lay off tens of thousands of employees because the slump in sales jeopardises a double-digit profit margin. Unemployment is often associated with exclusion and devaluation within society. The dependence on the community to finance the cost of living reduces self-esteem. Large-scale unemployment reduces the level of prosperity. Labour is an important element of prosperity for both the individual and the community. Moving away from a growth-orientated economy opens up the potential for a more stable community in which everyone participates in prosperity.

Globalization versus regionalization

We will remember the coronavirus pandemic for a longtime to come as the most devastating infectious disease since the Spanish flu. Not only because of the personal restrictions that people around the world have had to experience. The collapse of supply flows from Asia has dragged the entire global economy into a recession. Urgently needed components and other consumer goods were suddenly no longer available. Production facilities in the recipient countries came to a standstill. The pandemic has made the weak points of the global division of labour system painfully visible. The urge to relocate production facilities as workbenches of rich industrialised nations to countries with low location costs in order to remain competitive and guarantee high returns for investors has turned bitterly into a disadvantage and brought geostrategic dependencies into focus. The war against Ukraine, which has now been going on for two years and was started by Russia, as well as Israel's gruelling battle against the Palestinian terrorist organization Hamas after their massacre of over a thousand Israelis on 7 October 2023, on the highest Jewish holiday Yom Kippur, have once again brought the global supply system to a standstill.

The collapse of international supply chains particularly affects countries with few natural resources of their own and a high proportion of imports. Germany experienced a wave of shock after Russia stopped supplying gas at the end of 2022 in response to sanctions due to the attack on Ukraine. In the previous year, the share of cheap Russian gas imports was still 51 per cent.[86] German heating systems threatened to remain cold in the winter of 2022/2023 and the lack of industrial gas jeopardised jobs. The price of gas briefly exploded to four times its pre-crisis level. The Republic was shaken. In the end, the worst-case scenarios did not materialise due to rapid political countermeasures. In addition, mild winter temperatures and appeals to save energy caused consumption in 2023 to fall by 17.5 per cent compared to the four-year average for 2018-2021; industrial customers saved over 18 per cent and household and commercial customers over 16 per cent on gas.[87]

The golden decades of globalisation, driven by China's enormous economic upswing, seem to be over, at least for the time being. Europe's Supply Chain Act and the USA's Uyghur Forced Labour Prevention Act (UFLPA) are forcing companies to re-evaluate their location and supplier policies. Since the UFLPA came into force, US Customs has detained over 7,000 shipments worth almost four billion dollars on suspicion of forced labour by

Muslim Uyghurs. These include 13,000 luxury cars from the VW Group worth almost one billion euros. 71 Chinese companies have been placed on a blacklist.[88] Products containing components from these manufacturers are not allowed to be imported into the USA. Whether for political reasons directed against China or for humanitarian reasons, the US Congress is not only targeting European companies. In the summer of 2023, the US Congress launched an investigation into Ford. Ford had announced a partnership with the Chinese battery manufacturer CATL. Lithium-ion batteries use cobalt, which is mined in the Congo by Chinese mine operators under questionable working conditions. Ford withdrew from the joint venture shortly after the investigations began.[89] Tesla and BYD are already using lithium iron phosphate batteries that do not require cobalt.[90]

In addition to the geopolitical risks, there are also increasing location risks associated with climate change. As described in the previous chapters, global warming is leading to a massive change in climatic conditions in the various regions of the world. The scientists of the Intergovernmental Panel on Climate Change have developed very reliable simulations of greenhouse gas effects. In the most probable scenario from today's perspective (SSP2-4.5[9]) the earth will heat up by 2.1 to 3.5 degrees Celsius by the end of this century compared to the pre-

---

[9] SSPx-y = Socio economic pathway (socio-economic development path; x = model number; y = W/m^2 = radiation intensity in watts per square meter)

industrial period (1850 to 1900). The 2-degree threshold will therefore be exceeded between 2041 and 2060. The scientists of Working Group I of the Intergovernmental Panel on Climate Change classify this event as *extremely probable* under the assumptions of the above-mentioned model variant of the socio-economic pathway.

The consequences are more frequent and more intense rainfall and flood disasters, especially in Africa and Asia. Significantly more regions in North America, the Pacific Islands and Europe will also be affected by these natural events. The climatic drivers will intensify. The number of Floods and tropical cyclones will increase significantly. Their impact will be much more destructive. At 2 degrees Celsius and higher global warming, more frequent and longer phases of dryness and drought are also predicted. This will affect various regions in Africa, South America and Europe.[91] It is also likely to lead to an increase in dry periods in Australasia, Central and North America and the Caribbean. The website of the Intergovernmental Panel on Climate Change, www.ipcc.org, contains specific analyses of the five model variants for several regions.

For companies, the predictions of the Intergovernmental Panel on Climate Change's 6th Assessment Report mean that the reliability of global procurement channels will decrease to the extent that climate policy measures are further delayed. Every year that we fail to drastically reduce the biggest drivers of global warming, CO_2 and methane, the risk of global networking for procurement and sales increases. The risk affects the various industries and producers to very different degrees. The healthcare sector, medical and safety technology and disaster prevention may even benefit from these developments to some extent. The consumer goods and food industries will have to incorporate more far-reaching changes into their strategic considerations.

Even if the scientists do not come to the same conclusion on all points, the results are sufficient enough to seriously incorporate the scenarios into the strategic decision-making processes of company managers. Today's suppliers may no longer exist tomorrow, transport routes may be interrupted or no longer usable forever, sales markets may no longer exist. Some readers of these lines will object that entrepreneurs are and have always been exposed to such developments. The difference between the scenarios described and the past lies in their dynamism, global extent and intensity.

The regionalisation of value chains reduces capital requirements, reduces resource consumption and the climate footprint and strengthens social cohesion. As Dirk Posse points out, localisation also helps to reduce the pressure to grow.[92]

Increasing corporate value with sustainability

What would happen if a company decided today to stop growing? To preserve the status quo, to maintain the jobs provided in the long term, possibly to ensure a solidly secured company pension scheme, to maintain stable supplier relationships for many years to come? Such companies are very likely to become more attractive to employees, suppliers and customers. After all, they promise security and reliability for all stakeholders. No stress about losing your job at the next dip in sales. No need to worry about having to renegotiate the procurement contract every year - stability of the supply situation for both sides. All parties can relax and concentrate on the sustainable development of products, processes and customer loyalty. No dependency of quarterly reports with short-sighted performance indicators. The focus of these companies is on protecting the environment, preserving the surrounding habitat, a happy living community, regenerative economic activity and the conservation of biodiversity. That sounds very utopian. Such companies are quickly eaten up by competition. And yet there are more and more such companies that have taken up the cause of sustainable corporate management. Rebuy has been specialising in the repair and refurbishment of used electronic devices for 20 years and is holding its own in the market against all odds. Recently, however, it has had to fight against low-cost giants such as Temu or Shein from China. The EU's planned mandatory repair law encourages the company's founders to have made a far-sighted decision early on. Trigema is another German example that is known for standing by its employees even in difficult times and procuring its primary products regionally as far as possible. Patagonia can be cited as a prime example of sustainable corporate development. Yvion Chouinard and Tom Frost, both enthusiastic climbers and founders of Patagonia's predecessor - Chouinard Equipment for mountaineering gear - developed the spreader hook in 1972 after realising that the climbing hooks they were in great demand for were permanently damaging the mountains they admired, both when they were hammered in and when they came loose. To this day, Yvion Chouinard is committed to environmental protection and knows only one shareholder, Mother Earth.

One reason why there are still few companies that follow the example of Yvion Chouinard and the numerous small pioneers who have to fight for their existence lies in the intrinsic self-reinforcing powers of the growth system practiced. The financing of the company is one of the driving factors in this context. Financiers look very closely at the economic development of a borrower. Companies that grow steadily are also expected to be able to generate positive cashflows and profits in the future in order to repay their liabilities as agreed. The projection of future cash inflows is usually based on the earnings figures of the recent past and the current balance sheet. The growth rates are based on the assumed market development, the industrial sector and the company's own estimates of competitiveness. This framework of figures can quickly collapse if the estimated market and general conditions do not materialise or even collapse completely, as outlined above. Listed corporations are particularly exposed to growth pressure. So-called growth stocks are often valued at an above-average - sometimes even astronomical - price/earnings ratio and attract investors like flies to dung. The future development of the company's business activities, the market or the sector is factored into the valuation to a disproportionately high degree. In this way, start-ups manage to raise billions to finance their vision in a short space of time, even though they burn the money like straw. Only a few of these start-ups labelled as "unicorns" actually manage to build a permanently profitable business. The slightest doubt about the promises made causes them to fall out of investors' favour like hot potatoes, relentlessly and without delay. Young companies listed on the stock exchange can lose hundreds of millions of euros in value within minutes. Highly valued tech giants can lose billions in the same time. Those who have to put themselves in the shackles of covenants from their financiers – banks, private financiers, investors – due to financial bottlenecks have usually already lost the game. The loan and bond conditions stipulate what the creditor must do and refrain from doing during the agreed term of the loan in order to ensure repayment of the financing amount. This considerably restricts the company's ability to act. Patagonia has been no different in its corporate history. The team around YvonChouinard, which tirelessly developed improved and innovative products, achieved rapid sales growth. At the end of the 1980s, Inc. magazine listed it as the fastest growing private company. In 1991, the run was brought to an abrupt halt by an economic downturn. Sales collapsed and the banks called in the credit lines. Patagonia had to lay off 20 per cent of its closest employees in order to remain solvent. Patagonia had become a victim of its own growth hype. The management took this event as an opportunity to reflect on its original values and corporate culture and survived the crisis. Initially donating ten per cent of its profits, the company donates one per cent of its turnover to social and environmental projects every year, regardless of whether it makes a profit or a loss. With the "One per cent for the Planet Initiative", it also won over other companies to this idea. It was the first company in the USA to set up a company kindergarten so that employees could spend their lunch break with their children. Today, there are thousands of such facilities.[93] Patagonia is a good example of how a small company can stand up to the mainstream and make a big impact.

Today, investors and lenders pay closer attention to whether a company not only writes environmental protection and sustainability into its corporate code of conduct, but also implements them in its daily business. Under the environmental conditions described above, an active commitment to sustainability makes a significant contribution to reducing the risk of financing. Investments in sustainable companies are now not only favoured by the world's largest asset manager, Blackrock.

Investments in green technologies and "green" companies are also becoming increasingly popular with private investors. After all, they give hope that the path of environmental destruction we have embarked upon can be halted and the basis of life preserved for tomorrow. It is therefore to be expected that these creditors will still exist in a hundred years' time, which significantly increases their business value. Higher enterprise value and lower operating risk thus find their financiers and comparably more favourable financing conditions than their competitors, who continue to chase short-term success.

"The wind of change", once sung by the Scorpions at the fall of the Berlin Wall between East and West Germany, is blowing ever stronger. Sustainability, geopolitics and climate change will determine our future actions. There is little point in resisting them. In the face of rapidly advancing technical and digital developments, companies are called upon to adapt to future market conditions at an early stage. The best way to do this is to take the time to scrutinise and sharpen the company's "purpose" and derive a new vision and mission from it. Such an endeavour leads to reflection on the company and ownership structure, position in the social context, corporate culture, working and production methods, core activities, the company's capital requirements and how these are procured, as well as the required return on capital.

At the end of the process, we should find a company that is in harmony with the ecosystem in which it operates and is therefore more resilient to crises and able to adapt more quickly to change. A future-proof company.

Rethinking the economy

The dogma of constant growth does not stand up to intensive scrutiny in the long term. Is it not conceivable that a company might earn just a little more for its goods and merchandise than they cost it? Profit is measured by how much the entrepreneur needs to make new investments, raise new capital and develop new products and solutions. The aim of his business activities is not to maximise profits, but to meet the needs of his target markets. The shareholder value approach has led large corporations to align their profits and business activities with the return expected by shareholders, which should be in double figures if possible. It can be questioned whether a division with a profit margin of less than twelve per cent or higher is unprofitable and therefore tens of thousands of employees have to be laid off, or whether the preservation of jobs should not be valued more highly in favour of the social contribution to general satisfaction, and whether the co-owners would be satisfied with a lower return. In this context, it is interesting to note that the so-called dividend aristocrats, the name given to companies that have paid a dividend for 25 years or more without interruption, generally pay out little more than one per cent of the company's capital value each year.

Anders Indset states in his book "Quantum Economy": "The old system is no longer compatible with the new technologies."[94]

He is referring to the rapid progress of digitalisation. The point is made. Our previous understanding of economic activity and the purpose and aim of corporate management no longer fits today's framework conditions. While the disruptive effect of digitalisation, the development of quantum computers and the use of artificial intelligence is gradually dawning on us that there are also considerable risks lurking for our social development, we are still surprisingly unaffected by accelerated climate change and its devastating consequences.

In his book "Prosperity without Growth" - the update - Tim-Jackson recalls the essay by John Maynard Keynes, who is often cited by politicians and economists to justify their actions. In the midst of the global economic crisis triggered in 1929, accompanied by high mass unemployment, Keynes predicted in his essay "The Economic Possibilities of Our Grandchildren", published in 1930, that the economic problem would be solved 100 years later. By 2030, technical and economic development would have progressed so far that no-one would have to fear for their livelihood. Instead of having to fight for a living, people would then have enough time to look after their fellow human beings. The challenge will be to make sensible use of the free time gained. Keynes concludes that the economic problem, the daily struggle to make a decent living, will be almost overcome in 100 years and will therefore not be a permanent problem. In other words, the economic model of that time and today is only a transitional phase. However, the reflex developed over thousands of years of having to fight and work for our food and survival makes it difficult for us to break away from the ingrained rituals of getting on with our daily lives, accumulating wealth, continuously growing and having to generate even more returns.

Keynes' vision will hardly materialise in full by 2030. To some extent, however, prosperity in western industrialised nations has come very close to his prediction. In the heyday of industrialisation, the daily working time in Germany was often 14 to 16 hours with a six-day week. This also applied to children who were able to work.[95] The "Keynes vision" of working only three hours a day to satisfy the old instincts must have seemed unimaginable.

In the new era, the accumulation of material values will no longer play a role. The fulfilment of life will be determined by the extent to which everyone succeeds in making a contribution to their social environment. Social recognition is no longer defined by the accumulation of material goods, but by the wealth experienced through positive feedback from the social environment.

Post-growth equals zero growth

What should such a new economic system look like? And how can we achieve this transformation? Some aspects have been addressed in the previous chapters. As the author has already pointed out several times, limiting renewable resources and energy must be at the centre of future economic activity. We should only consume as much in one period as we can recover in terms of basic material and nutrients in the same time. This principle certainly makes sense to the Swabian housewife. The (organic) farmer also cultivates his fields in such a way that they enable a regular yield and do not deplete the soil on which he ultimately lives.

In the various scientific publications that deal with an alternative economic model, the term post-growth society or a post-growth model has become established. The limitation of growth, as derived in the previous chapters, simply results from the realisation that non-renewable resources are only available to a limited extent on this planet, the limited regenerative capacity of certain goods (food, arable land) and the need to put a stop to climate-damaging behaviour - the sooner the better. Today, measures to delay climate change are at the top of the political agenda. First and foremost is the reduction of greenhouse gas emissions. So would it be enough to reorganize the economy in such a way that net emissions of CO_2 and methane are reduced to zero and, as assumed in the SSP1-1.9 model of the IPPC's 6th Assessment Report, additionally to remove greenhouse gas from the atmosphere? The answer to this question is a clear "no". The very important discussions about climate change and the indispensable appeals to become aware of its consequences must not obscure the fact that we are facing a fundamental social challenge. On the one hand, there is the overexploitation of natural resources and the destruction of biodiversity triggered by consumerist excesses. On the other hand, we face the ever-increasing imbalance between wealthy, affluent regions and the majority of the world's poor population. The material orientation of society and its understanding of prosperity is also clearly not leading to greater satisfaction and cohesion of its members. Our experience of the people of the barren fjord landscape in the north of Norway is very different. When a young Swedish travel guide was asked why he would choose to live and work in the sparsely populated Tromsø in northern Norway when he could have so much more variety at home, he replied: "People are friendly here, they help each other, they know each other. If I want to buy a new computer, I have to drive three hours west and there might not be anyone available. Life is quieter here and closer to nature." The human relationship with each other is more important there than the exuberant diversity in the satellite towns, where people are increasingly alienated from each other in densely built tenements.

So, can there be no more growth at all under the assumptions described? If we look at the macroeconomic level of the earth system as a whole, then it is clear that growth can only take place to the extent that renewable sources of raw materials allow it or we find less limited substitutes. On the other hand, growth is only possible if some actors reduce their consumption in the ecosystem and make it available to those who have not yet reached an adequate level of prosperity. In a free market economy, as we assume in this book, there will always be companies that can gain market share because competitors drop out of the market or they serve a market that has not yet been discovered by a competitor. Low-material service providers, for example in the care of the elderly and sick, in art institutions and other service sectors, still have growth potential for a long time to come. From the author's point of view, the term "post-growth economy" is therefore easily misleading. What is certain is that we are looking for a form of economy that turns away from the excessive primacy of growth and emphasises the social orientation of economic activity.

Social performance instead of Material throughput

For this we need a new, but at least complementary, primary measure of an economy's performance instead of gross national product, which is geared towards high material throughput. We can find ideas for this in happiness research. The Gross Happiness Index (GHI), for example, measures the psychological well-being of society in addition to material prosperity.[96] The GHI has its origin in the Kingdom of Bhutan. Iceland, New Zealand, Scotland and Wales, as well as Australia, also follow the GHI principle. The United Arab Emirates has even set up its own Ministry of Happiness to develop a happy and contented population. The Bhutanese concept comprises four dimensions:

- o Promoting equitable social and economic development,
- o Preservation and promotion of cultural values,

- Protection of the environment,
- good government and administrative structures.

The four measurement areas are assigned 33 indicators that are surveyed nationwide at regular intervals.[97]

The United Nations has been publishing the World Happiness Report (WHR) since 2011 on the initiative of the then Prime Minister of Bhutan, Jigme Thinley. It currently covers more than 140 countries and ranked Finland in first place in 2023, followed by Denmark and Iceland. Germany ranks 16th [10] among the happiest people in the world.[98] The ranking is based on six metrics: gross national product per capita, level of social support, life expectancy, self-determination to shape one's own life, willingness to help others and the absence of corruption. Bhutan was ranked 97th in the 2017 report; there is no information on Bhutan in the World Happiness Report 2023. Objectifying life satisfaction is not an easy endeavour. Bhutanese may feel much happier than the WHR would suggest.

In search of an alternative to GDP, the German Bundestag setup an Enquete Commission on 1 December 2010. The commission was tasked with investigating the question of how social prosperity, individual well-being and sustainable development can be appropriately defined and depicted in a society.[99]

---

[10] In the WHR 2024, which was published shortly before this book was finalised, Germany drops to 24th place in the ranking. The USA falls from 15th place (2023) to 23rd.

Among other things, the 62 members of the Commission were tasked with "developing a holistic indicator of prosperity or progress and exploring the possibilities and limits of decoupling growth, resource use and technological progress."[100] Despite the sometimes very different, party political positions of the parliamentarians and experts Daniela Kolbe, working group's chairwoman, stated that "a surprisingly far-reaching consensus was achieved."[101] However, this statement also indicates the difficulty that the Commission's Project Group 2 faced in defining a prosperity indicator. Different value judgements and world views, ethical and political factors do not make it easy to select generally accepted, reliable and internationally comparable indicators. After two years of work, an expanded GDP was proposed, which includes ten leading indicators from three dimensions:

- o Material prosperity:
   + Per capita income
   + Income distribution
   + Public Debt

- o Social affairs/participation:
   + Employment
   + Education
   + Health
   + Freedom

    o   Ecology
        + Greenhouse gases
        + Nitrogen
        + Biodiversity

The Enquete Commission's wish to publicise the W3-indicators and stimulate social debate about them has not been fulfilled. The author was not able to find any corresponding status reports or the recommended interactive website on the metrics.[102] It seems as if the parliamentarians' findings and proposals have sunk into the Bundestag archives. At the presentation of the 2021 Annual Economic Report, the incumbent Minister of Economic Affairs, Robert Habeck, presented 31 alternative indicators for measuring prosperity.[103] He could have used the National Welfare Index (NWI), developed in 2009 by Hans Diefenbacher, Roland Zieschank and Dorothee Rodenhäuser on behalf of the Federal Environment Agency, which the Enquete Commission had also included in its deliberations.[104] In its current version, the NWI 3.0 comprises 21 components that are included in the calculation of the index in monetary form.[105] Starting with the private consumer spending six welfare-creating indicators are added and 15 welfare-reducing metrics are subtracted. The NWI measures the development of prosperity in Germany based on available data from 1991 onwards and compares this with the simultaneous development of gross domestic product (GDP). From 1991 to 1999, the NWI shows an increase in welfare measurement in line with GDP. It then fell by a good ten per cent to remain virtually unchanged at this level until 2013, while GDP continued its rise, only briefly slowed by the 2008/2009 financial crisis. In the following years, the NWI was also able to increase again slightly until the coronavirus pandemic hit. While GDP recovered quickly after the global lung disease was contained and reached a new high in 2021, the NWI fell again significantly. According to the Federal Environment Agency, stagnating income inequality and rising environmental costs are offsetting increases in consumer spending. Most recently, the flood disaster on the Ahr and Erft rivers (2021) led to a further drop in the national welfare indicator.[106] The NWI, which also exists at the level of some federal states as a Regional Welfare Indicator (RWI), like other methodological approaches to measuring prosperity, is not free from criticism and is not without its limitations. A basic assumption of the NWI is the positive effect of increases in consumption on prosperity and quality of life. As explained in the previous chapters, this is only the case to a certain extent. One could introduce a cap on the influencing variable, as assumed by Daniel Kahneman and Angus Deaton, for example. Or a degression curve that runs towards zero. It is also difficult to assess environmental damage or the social consequences of road accidents. For example, there is the question of how greenhouse gas emissions and their consequences should be priced. The developers of the "Welfare Index" concede that a positive trend in the NWI does not reveal, among other things, "whether a country's welfare development would be ecologically sustainable in the longer term, for example."[107] The development of a universal welfare indicator would be desirable. The objective measurability of the indicators must be a prerequisite for global acceptance. This requires a transparent and unambiguous definition and calculation of the components. Political influence, as with the indicator developed by the Enquete Commission or the Human Development Index (HDI) used by the United Nations, whose calculation method has been changed several times following diplomatic interventions, makes these appear unsuitable as globally recognised measures of prosperity. Nevertheless, the United Nations would probably be the most suitable institution to promote such a project. All politicians and experts who have looked at alternatives to GDP agree that the latter is not suitable for measuring prosperity and quality of life.

Efficiency-consistency-sufficiency

In our consideration of how a transformation of the status quo to a sustainable form of economy could succeed, it is crucial to what extent we can eliminate or neutralise the existing drivers of growth. Identified drivers of a growth trapped economy include competitive pressure, expected returns, financing, status consumption and long value chains. In the scientific discourse on escaping these constraints, three sustainability strategies have emerged that the state, society and companies should pursue within the scope of their influence.

The efficient use and handling of available resources and operating materials is the top priority. This strategy is primarily based on technical improvements to operating processes and innovations. The strategy is therefore mainly aimed at entrepreneurs and the state, insofar as the latter is involved in entrepreneurial activities. The endeavour to achieve maximum results with minimum effort is in the DNA of a company anyway. The reduction of waste quantities through sophisticated designs and improved production processes and the increased use of recycled materials are suitable means of increasing the efficiency of resources. Intelligent irrigation systems help to significantly reduce water consumption in agriculture. Creating products on-demand, as is possible with 3D printers, helps to reduce inventories, releases the capital tied up there and reduces the risk of old stock no longer finding a buyer and having to be disposed of. The electric car is considerably more efficient than the car equipped with a combustion engine - even if it is fueled with e-fuels. The efficiency of the pure battery-powered car of 73 per cent is also significantly higher than that of the hydrogen-powered alternative at 31 per cent. The combustion engine achieves a maximum technically possible 40 per cent. In practice, however, it only achieves a little more than half of this.[108] The battery-electric drive is also clearly ahead in the overall eco-balance. Producers and consumers need to be made much more aware of the value of natural resources in particular - which is often not represented by the price. Companies and institutions that are doing pioneering work in this area should receive more support. Digitalisation and artificial intelligence

Fundamentals of the economy of tomorrow

Keynes probably did not realise that technological progress and population growth would mean that we would use up resources faster than they could be regenerated. Moreover, that the resulting environmental damage would lead to a reduction in habitats and could jeopardise the food supply. But this is precisely the scenario we are facing today - less than seven years before the end of the 100 years predicted by Keynes.

We will not be able to develop a complete new economic model in this book. That is not the aim. Rather, it is important to understand that we need a new economic model. The French economist and philosopher François Quesnay (1694 to1774) coined the term laissez-fair economics, on the basis of which Adam Smith developed the concept of a free market economy. Karl Marx and Friedrich Engels developed the model of socialism in the face of exploitative entrepreneurship in the era of industrialisation. Instead of placing the means of production in the hands of a few self-indulgent private entrepreneurs and landlords, the collective was to decide on their use and, above all, the remuneration of the labour force, thus leading to a classless society. Ludwig Erhard, German Federal Minister of Economics from 1949 to 1963, is regarded as the father of the social market economy. It combined the ideas of a free market economy with social and controlling elements that were the responsibility of the state. The interests of the private sector, socio-political norms and social security were to be balanced by the state. In none of the economic models mentioned, which are practised in different forms around the world, are the aspects of sustainability and a balanced ecosystem or the limited availability of raw materials really ascribed any value. However, based on the knowledge available, we should be able to find a fourth way that makes prosperity, social justice and sustainable economic activity equally possible.

The cornerstones of a sustainable further development of economic principles are a service-oriented society, greater regionalisation of value chains and a modernised financial system.

In an economy without growth, service plays an essential and greater role than it does today. We have already addressed this aspect in the chapter on the sustainable company. In future, the value of a company could be measured by the social and socio-economic contribution it makes. Sustainability and environmental compatibility will become differentiating evaluation factors.

A stronger focus of the economy on the principle of service contributes to absorbing the labour force made redundant by technological progress. Robotics and AI are driving the use of light-out manufacturing. Empty factories where robots do the work. The advantages are obvious. Robots no heating, ventilation or air conditioning. Rejects and downtime at the workstations are reduced and productivity increases. Unit costs are significantly reduced and justify the high investments still required today. The Japanese company FANUC has long relied on the black factory, in which only robots work. In 2020, Amazon had more than 200,000 mobile robots in use to support work processes in its logistics centres. Quantum computers will exponentially accelerate the digitalisation and use of AI to reduce the workload for human workers. While commercially available 3D printers were initially used for hobby purposes, similar to the popularity of home computers such as the Commodore C64, the technology is now being used to digitally build entire houses. Not only is this technology speeding up the construction of new homes, it is also eliminating numerous direct and indirect jobs. Instead of carrying out complex and time-consuming measurements and tests during building construction, in future it may be sufficient to certify the software and the materials used alone.

Not only will the number of people employed in the manufacturing sector in developed economies fall sharply, but jobs will shift from simple activities to demanding control and development tasks. The education system has a key role to play on the road to the future. The job profile in the manufacturing industry of tomorrow, as well as in some sectors of the service industry, requires well-trained specialists and technicians, programmers and developers. Even with the best education system, not all people who are able to work will be able to fulfil the requirements profile of demanding jobs in manufacturing and services. However, even though self-propelled serving machines are already finding their way into the catering industry, not all tasks will be performed by robots in the future. Nor is this desirable. "Humans are irreplaceable!" said Rudolf Karazman, founder of IBG Innovatives Betriebliches Gesundheitsmanagement GmbH, in a 2016 lecture on the topic of the humanless factory. In the production of the future, employees will be consciously integrated into all relevant processes of the smart factory as experts and decision makers.[113] There is therefore hope that the shortage of skilled workers identified in Germany is only temporary. Politicians would be well advised not to overshoot the mark with their remedial measures. Otherwise, we can expect a surplus of skilled labour in a few years' time. A situation like the one we experienced for decades in teacher training. A recent study by the Bertelsmann Foundation comes to the conclusion that the current shortage of primary schoolteachers will be resolved sooner than expected. Instead, education researchers expect a surplus of primary schoolteachers by 2035. This is due to demographic developments. The Conference of German Education Ministers came to a very different conclusion in its projections.[114]

Strengthening the service sector firstly reduces the need for continued productivity increases in order to absorb cost increases. Some services are even immune to efficiency gains. In the case of healthcare services, childcare or the arts, it is the quality of the work performed that counts. The time factor becomes a marker of quality. Many services cannot be provided any faster or with fewer staff. A service-orientated economy can contribute to maintaining full employment and have a positive impact on the perception of welfare. The economist William Baumol has extensively researched the service sector. He came to the conclusion that the growth of a service-orientated economy tends towards zero in the long term.[115] And, as already mentioned, with a high level of employment. His considerations are supported by empirical research.

Sustainable Finance

If the pursuit of profit is no longer at the centre of the new economy, but rather the social contribution to the common good, it is obvious that the financial markets will also play a different role. The question arises as to whether speculation will still be desired or permitted in a future global economy. How does it benefit the economy when securities jugglers sell short? In other words, selling shares that they do not even own in order to buy them at a later date, thanks to a successful bet, at a lower price than agreed at the time of speculation? Speculation with structured derivatives based on multiple bundles of non-transparent bonds, which were the cause of the 2007/2008 financial crisis, does not provide any recognizable benefit according to ESG-criteria[13], but does pose a threat to the economic system. The global domino effect set in motion by the closely interlinked banking system has alarmed politicians, economists

---

[13] ESG stands for Environment, Social and Governance

and regulators alike. Is it ethical and socially acceptable for food and basic goods to be the subject of speculation? High inflation as a result of the Russia-Ukraine war in 2022/2023 has alarmed politicians in the European Union. Even in the seemingly stable democracies, the loss of energy supplies and galloping inflation with a simultaneous drop in production and rising unemployment would lead to social unrest with unforeseeable consequences. Price caps and hundreds of billions of euros in relief packages were launched in 2022 to prevent the worst from happening.

The money and financial markets will continue to play an important role in the new economic world. Flats, houses and large investments will still need to be financed. However, it is important to orientate financing towards sustainability and to check whether it makes a positive contribution to a sustainable ecosystem.

Up to now, investments have been based on parameters such as future growth rates, profit expectations and the price/earnings ratio - all growth indicators. If a listed company does not fulfil expectations, the shares are quickly pushed downwards. In a world in which growth is no longer the decisive benchmark, things should be much calmer on the capital markets. Equities could then behave more like bonds. Stable earnings ensure reliable returns. As described in the chapter "The sustainable company", the risk of a company operating sustainably in this sense is significantly lower than that of its growth-driven competitors. This is particularly true if the latter utilise environmentally harmful technologies and processes. The European Union has enacted a transparency law in the form of the Taxonomy Regulation which contains criteria for determining the degree of environmental sustainability of an investment.[116] In addition to environmental aspects, social requirements and corporate governance criteria are also included.

An investment is only considered environmentally sustainable if minimum standards for labour and human rights are met. The so-called ESG criteria are decisive for the German Federal Financial Supervisory Authority (Bafin) when assessing the risk of the financial service providers it commissions. The EU Sustainable Finance Disclosure Regulation (SFDR), which came into force in March 2021, requires financial market participants and financial advisors to comprehensively disclose information relating to the sustainability of the investment. Since August 2022, providers of investment products have also been obliged to ask their customers about their sustainability preferences.[117] Since 2022, insurance companies and pension funds have been required to include sustainability risks in their risk management and take long-term climate change scenarios into account.

The observable threat to biodiversity and the decline in ecosystem services is increasingly being recognised as a systemic risk by companies and investors.[118] The loss of biodiversity poses a particular threat to the food supply. Various non-governmental organisations are working on a reporting standard to make the risk of corporate activities in relation to ESG criteria transparent and comparable. The Corporate Sustainability Reporting Directive (CSRD) has been in force within the European Union since January 2023. This obliges all large companies and all listed corporations, with the exception of micro-enterprises, to report on the risks and opportunities of social and environmentally relevant events and their impact on people and the environment. Both the external impact and events that jeopardise the company itself must be taken into account. The reporter must therefore disclose its influence on the environment in the broadest sense, as well as its dependencies on the environment. This is referred to as double materiality.[119] The CSRD is supplemented by the Corporate Sustainability Due Diligence Directive (CSDDD or CS3D), which has already been discussed.

The initiatives of the European Union and at international level, including the IFRS Foundation [14] suggest that the requirements for environmentally friendly and sustainable behaviour will extend even further to the capital markets themselves. Sustainability reports are important information for company evaluation by rating agencies. In future, sustainable corporate governance will have a significant influence on creditworthiness and the investment grade, which ultimately determines whether the company finds investors and on what terms. In the Fi-

---

[14] The International Financial Reporting Standards (IFRS) are the most widely recognised international accounting standards for companies

nance for Biodiversity Initiative, financial institutions from 26 countries have joined forces and committed to contributing to the protection, conservation and restoration of the natural ecosystem through their financial activities and investments.[120]

Criticism of the current financial system is fuelled by the trend towards unequal distribution of wealth. Low key interest rates set by central banks tempt the state and companies, to take out more loans in order to expand their investments. It is cheap money. We have highlighted the consequences of this debt trap in the chapter on the glut of money. On the other hand, savings are losing value. The low interest on savings is eaten up by inflation. In real terms, assets are falling. This primarily affects small savers and pensioners, whose retirement provisions will not be sufficient to maintain their accustomed standard of living after retirement. Insurance companies and pension funds, which until now have been an important pillar of retirement provision, are affected to the same extent.

At this point, we would like to emphasise that in the course of the transformation process of the economy towards sustainability and the preservation of the natural ecosystem, as well as the necessary social change, we cannot avoid adapting the current financial and monetary system. The source of the glut of money that was mentioned results from the fact that banks in today's world can grant loans without having corresponding deposits available on the other side. This means that banks are authorised to create money out of nothing. In financial accounting terms, this is how it looks: On the assets side of the balance sheet, the bank enters a receivable in the amount of the loan; on the liabilities side of the balance sheet, a deposit in the same amount is entered as an offsetting entry. In this way, the bank can greatly inflate its statement of assets. Like a magician, the bank has thus increased the amount of money in circulation out of nothing. It is not surprising that financial experts and economists have long been thinking about how to remedy the disadvantages of this debt-based monetary system.

A much-discussed idea originated from the American economic researcher Irving Fisher. He developed the so-called Chicago Plan. This stipulates that every bank deposit must be covered 100 per cent by central bank money. Jaromir Benes and his colleague Michael Kumhof worked out the advantages of this proposal as part of an International Monetary Fund working paper.[121] The credit-based economic cycles can be brought under better control. Bank runs can be avoided. Both government debt and private debt will fall drastically. Control of the money supply would once again be in the hands of a centralised public institution, i.e. the state - as with the mint - and no longer with the banks. In their state-of-the-art model of a central bank money-backed system, Benes and Kumhof also identified the advantages that there would be no liquidity bottlenecks and inflation would be close to zero in the long term.[122] Benes and Kumhof's working paper triggered a fierce debate about the pros and cons of the Chicago Plan. It is hardly surprising that the Federal Bank of Germany does not think much of it.[123] It is obvious that there is enormous resistance also to this topic. Experts in their field argue on both sides. Politicians of all colours are not yet prepared to initiate such a far-reaching reform of the financial and monetary system.

It doesn't work without change

Centuries of industrialisation have brought people a high level of material prosperity, especially in the market-oriented Western regions. Some of the developing countries look enviously at the richly laid table of the so-called industrialised countries. The dishwashing careers that generated millionaires for young professionals from poor backgrounds are the model for many generations from the world's poor neighbourhoods. The New Economy has even turned students into billionaires in a short space of time with its innovative start-ups. The "unicorn" - a young company that achieves a company valuation of one billion dollars in short financing rounds - is the new idol to be emulated. The unicorn concept is based on an innovative idea and an aggressive growth strategy. Losses are compensated for in new rounds of financing and with the further expansion of the business model. However, only a few companies actually manage to break even; Tesla is a positive example of this.

Who is joining in?

People stick to roads and runways. They smear the walls of government buildings with black liquid, throw mashed potatoes at valuable paintings and disrupt cultural events. It is the outcry of the "Last Generation", as the rebels call themselves, an alliance of climate activists from Germany, Austria and Italy.[124]

TV programmes, radio news, print and social media outdo each other daily with new bad news. The ocean off Florida reaches bathtub temperature, an unprecedented forest fire rages in Greece and forces people into their homes. The USA groaned under unbearable heat in the summer of 2023. As did people in southern and central Europe. Experts are warning of the consequences of the climate catastrophe in increasingly shrill tones. And yet it seems as if the warning signals are only reaching the population muffled, as if through cotton wool balls in their ears. Are we so preoccupied with ourselves that the outside world no longer concerns us? Have we become so self-absorbed and disconnected from nature that we no longer recognise the changes on this planet, or - to protect ourselves from the prosperity we have achieved - do not want to acknowledge them?

António Guterres never tires of appealing. But is anyone listening to him? The Secretary-General of the United Nations appears to be the lone admonisher in the desert. Although the 193 member states have all committed themselves to the 17 Sustainable Development Goals and have pledged to actively implement them in their countries through national laws and regulations. By 2030, poverty and hunger are to be eradicated in the world, sustainable measures to combat climate change are to be implemented and peace and justice are to be ensured throughout the world. Today, in 2024, we are further away from achieving these goals than ever before. Keynes would shake his head in disappointment. After all, we are universally more technologically advanced than when he wrote his essay on the economic possibilities of our grandchildren. In 100 years - i.e.2030 - he assumed that the above goals will have been achieved as a result of economic and social development. So it can't be down to technical progress.

Powerful forces stand in the way of realising these ambitious commitments. Wherever we look, the quest for power and an unhealthy individualism have taken hold. In many countries, we are seeing a trend towards dictatorial governments whose rulers do not stop at the overexploitation of valuable and nonrecoverable resources in favour of personal gain. These autocrats are not the least bit interested in the hunger and misery of their own people. In Western nations, politicians seem to have lost their inner compass. More and more voters no longer feel understood and left alone with their problems. A common canon of values seems to have been lost.

The longing for a strong leading figure is driving more and more people into the arms of the so-called right-wing parties. They lure people in by trivialising and in some cases denying man-made climate change and its consequences, and cater to the desire of many people to be spared the catastrophes by simply ignoring them. Everything will not be so bad, they promise. Conservative Republican Donald Trump is ranting loudest on the world stage and is shaking up the seemingly dormant world order created after the Second World War. In his first term as President of the United States of America, Trump has cancelled hard-won international agreements on arms limitation, nuclear armament, norms and standards in global trade with the stroke of a pen. "America First", as his slogan goes, mobilises half of Americans with conspiracy theories, denial of the human made climate change, and declares the empirically proven facts of scientists who predict a catastrophic development of the earth's ecosystem to be fairy tales. In the end, Trump and his supporters are also only interested in realising their own egoism, power interests and maintaining personal, material prosperity, which, as already explained, is highly questionable. This state of affairs should definitely be preserved regardless of the living conditions of people in the rest of the world. An extremely dubious endeavour that is doomed to failure.

Influential industry associations and their lobbyists have no interest in changing the status quo that has brought them so much economic success. The German government's Building Energy Act, presented in the summer of 2023, has led the entire country to heated controversies and emotional arguments at the regulars' tables and in parliament. Instead of constructively ironing out the technical errors and lack of communication, the entire bill was demonised in the strongest possible terms. Although the intention and thrust are in line with European and national climate targets. Farmers' organisations oppose excessively strict climate protection laws, which they believe place too great a burden on farmers' incomes. Peatlands, which release CO_2 stored over millions of years by drying out, would have to be rewetted. However, this would be at the expense of livestock farming. The German car industry has long resisted further requirements to reduce particulate matter and CO_2 emissions, and has almost slept through the transition to electrified vehicles. VW has lost its decades-long dominant position in the Chinese car market to local start-ups and is struggling to regain ground.

The year 2023 was characterised by high inflation in all industrialised countries, rising interest rates following the wasteful glut of money in the post-financial crisis and the threat of recession after the coronavirus pandemic had just been overcome. Germany is even being dubbed the "sick man of Europe" by the media. And once again, the familiar reflex of calling for a government cash injection to get the stuttering economy back on its usual growth path is taking hold. Yet it could be a welcome opportunity to slow down the carousel of prosperity. Giving the free market the opportunity to adjust supply and demand to a significantly lower level. The restrictions imposed during the coronavirus pandemic have shown how positively the enforced restraint has impacted our ecosystem. But how are ordinary citizens supposed to come up with the idea of permanently reducing their consumption when renowned economists, government advisers and other supposedly knowledgeable experts are calling for growth stimuli as the sole recipe for countering the economic downturn via all available information channels? Scientists and economic experts who point out alternatives for maintaining our prosperity with low or zero growth are not present in the media landscape.

False role model

The primacy of economic growth seems to be carved in stone, like the ten commandments of Moses. Breaking this commandment is tantamount to anarchy. If the former colonial powers and western industrialised countries have succeeded in one thing in the long term, it is the global spread of the belief that only growth can guarantee prosperity and satisfaction of mankind. Even the 2030 Agenda of the United Nations reaffirms this in point 27 of its declaration: "sustainable economic growth is essential for prosperity" [125] For its part, the German Federal Government confirmed in 2023: "Sustainable economic growth is a basis for prosperity in Germany."[126] Sustainability and steady growth - how can they go together? In its final report in 2013, the Enquete Commission of the German Bundestag set up in 2010 stated that the political task of harmonising universal prosperity with a thriving state of our natural environment is made more difficult by the fact that "more and more people on our planet are orientating themselves towards the industrialised countries' understanding of prosperity, which is based on a huge consumption of resources and energy."[127]

The 193 signatories of the 2030 Agenda already state in the preamble to the declaration: "Economic, social and technological development must take place in harmony with nature. It is therefore necessary to fundamentally change the way we produce and consume goods and services. All socially relevant parties must contribute to changing unsustainable patterns of behaviour.[128] The 193 member states have committed themselves to very far-reaching changes in the way we live together on this planet. In this context, "sustainable" means that in the future - which starts six years from today (2024) - we will only consume as much as the planet makes available to us or can regenerate in one period. Let's stop overfishing the oceans as quickly as possible and give up Japanese delicacies. It is also not vital and not necessarily an indicator of prosperity to capture songbirds enmasse and to the spoilt Italian palate. Let's stop the overfertilisation and salinisation of the soil and cultivate our fields again in such a way that the soil has time to recover and rebuild used nutrients. Intelligent, sustainable agriculture, reforestation and the re-naturalisation of moors are essential to maintain our drinking water supply.

Growth should therefore only be granted to less developed economies. The German government has set an annual increase in gross domestic product of at least seven per cent for this group of countries, in order to equalize living conditions between the old and the new world.[129] However, the communiqué fails to define which countries fall under this category - as does the UN declaration.

This book does not want to join in the alarmism that is being fuelled by the attention-seeking media. On the other hand, we are already experiencing the environmental changes in our heated cities, flooded valleys and increasing storms in our everyday lives. The heatwave month of July 2023 made this clear worldwide. It doesn't help to bury our heads in the sand. We must adapt to the changing environmental conditions.

Juli Zeh has her protagonist in the novel "Über Menschen" think: "Why didn't she - Greta Thunberg - say: "I have a dream" instead of "How dare you?"[130] The tone makes the music. Let's follow a dream instead of being forced by shrill tones.

Closing remarks

Let's imagine we were in Alexander Gerst's shoes, looking down on our still blue planet from the ISS space station. Which, as the German space traveller admitted in one of his exciting lectures, he had little opportunity to do while conducting hundreds of experiments. From this great distance, we would realise that there are living beings on the round planet who, in a frenzy of consumption, are destroying everything that grows and thrives on this blue wonder faster than nature can restore it. We would also be able to observe that only a small part of this species down there exhibits such behaviour. The majority of the population obviously lives in much poorer conditions and struggles to survive on a daily basis. Almost a billion people do not have enough to eat, no clean water and live in poor accommodation. The life expectancy of these people is low, while the population living in abundance is producing more and more centenarians. From the dark perspective of space, we observe that the planet is continuously heating up. We should realise that global warming will continue until the middle of the century. This trend will continue into the 21st century, even if mankind takes immediate action worldwide to reduce greenhouse gas emissions and remove CO_2 from the atmosphere. Some of the effects of climate-determining factors will only have an impact after decades or centuries, in both directions. It is highly likely that we will miss the target of 1.5 degrees Celsius by

2030 and will barely manage to keep global warming below 2 degrees Celsius, as is possible under the SSP1-1.9 and SSP1-2.6 scenarios. We are currently on the SSP2-4.5 path with a calculated warming of the planet of between 2.1 and 3.5 degrees Celsius. The last time the blue planet experienced a warming of or above 2.5 degrees Celsius was more than three million years ago.[131] We are looking at increasingly frequent natural disasters that devastate large parts of the globe orbiting the sun and make it unsuitable for life. We think of the 6th Assessment Report of the Intergovernmental Panel on Climate Change[15] – from March 2023. With every half degree of global warming, the intensity and frequency of heat extremes and heatwaves increase. Especially in the north-eastern regions - Russia, Asia, North America, North Africa - and in the Arctic polar regions, unprecedentedly heavy rainfall will occur with increasing frequency. In large parts of Europe, South Africa, South America and South-East Asia, we are very likely to experience more frequent dry spells and droughts. From a warming of 1.5 degrees above the preindustrial age (1850 to 1900), scientists expect an increasing frequency of extreme events that has not occurred since they were recorded.[132] In the 19th century, heat events occurred on average every 50 years; today we experience them on average every ten years. From 1.5 degrees global warming,

---

[15] The IPCC was established in 1988 by the United Nations Environment Programme (UNEP) and the World Meteorological Organisation (WMO). More than 200 scientists and experts from around the world were involved in the four working groups that produced the 6th Assessment Report.

the frequency is classified as every six years with a high probability, and from 2 degrees these extreme events occur every four years.[133] Based on refined model calculations, scientists expect the Earth's surface temperature to be 1.5 degrees higher in the 2030s than it was between 1850 and 1900. 2023/2024 we are at approx. 1.1 degrees (plus/minus ten per cent) temperature increase measured over the entire planet. At an average of 1.59 degrees Celsius, the land regions are considerably hotter than the oceans at around 0.88 degrees. Another statement in the assessment report has caught our attention. The warming, acidification and oxygen depletion of the oceans caused by greenhouse gas emissions since 1750 cannot be reversed for hundreds to thousands of years.

Our observations can be summarised as follows: Despite enormous technological and medical advances, the way in which humans have managed the economy over the last 200 years has tended to increase regional and supra-regional inequality among the earth's population. There is ample evidence that this process will continue. At the same time, we are witnessing the continued destruction of our natural resources. Biodiversity is being destroyed to an extent that is highly unlikely to be reversed. The reduction of habitats due to climate change is leading to mass exodus to regions that are still worth living in. The constant increase in material wealth contributes less and less to an increased sense of prosperity. The marginal utility in relation to the perceived sense of prosperity reaches its maximum value at a certain level and generates more dissatisfaction than satisfaction. Certainly not everything was better in the past. Wars, diseases, natural disasters, misery and unemployment characterised the past centuries, which nobody wants to relive. But one or two people may remember a time when they had fewer financial resources, when roast dinners were only served on Sundays on the table and the fish was only available on Fridays. People were not any less satisfied because of this.

We experience a strong sense of community and the greatest feeling of happiness in our relationships with partners, friends, family and neighbours, in the recognition of our achievements by others or when we can make other people happy. These prosperity factors cannot be measured by the figures of gross national product. With a different focus on the life situation of a society, prosperity and satisfaction can be created and even increased, even without material growth.

We still have around ten years to prevent global warming from exceeding 1.5 degrees Celsius and the consequences from increasing exponentially. At the same time, we are rapidly approaching tipping points that will irretrievably destroy our ecosystem.

Let us be aware: prosperity does not come for free. It is wiser if we start reshaping the future now, while it is still in our hands.

Acknowledgement

It was a lucky coincidence that Tim Jackson's book fell into my hands. Perhaps it was also an unconscious search for an answer to the challenges we face. His study on the question of whether prosperity is possible without growth ultimately prompted me to write this book. In this respect, I would like to thank him for his inspiration.

But above all, I would like to thank Andreas Dripke, an accomplished writer, copywriter, author of numerous books and publications, entrepreneur and Chairman of the Diplomatic Council (UN reg.). After my first attempt at writing as a co-author, he encouraged me to continue and inspired me to write this book. Our conversations were valuable reflections and gave me the impetus to look at the issues and proposed solutions described from other perspectives. Afterall, there is not just one solution to this complex issue, not just one way.

It is important to keep the goal in mind. I would like to thank the editors of Diplomatic Council Publishing for their efforts in tracking down the errors and the publisher for the successful design of this work. Of course, my wife should not go unmentioned at this point. She had my back and, with a great deal of understanding, gave me the time I needed for the months of research and subsequent writing.

I dedicated the book to my sons.

In the hope that you, dear readers, and I will pave the way for a sustainable future worth living in for them and all the other sons, daughters and grandchildren of this world. For this I thank you in advance.

About the author

Helmut von Siedmogrodzki was born in Düsseldorf in 1955, studied computer science and graduated in economics and organisational sciences. After a successful career as an officer in the German Armed Forces and 23 years in a world leading German industrial group as Managing Director, CFO and Director of Boards in China, Hong Kong and Taiwan, he became self-employed in 2010. Since then, he has been advising medium-sized companies on their investments in China and the Middle East with his company Siebenburg International.

He has lived and worked in China since 1997 and spent several years in the United Arab Emirates. As Chairman International Relations of the Diplomatic Council (DC), he supports the development of the DC in the UAE and the People's Republic of China.

Helmut von Siedmogrodzki has been involved in the topic of sustainable corporate management and economic growth for many years. He regularly organises discussion evenings on current economic and technological developments. He is a much sought-after speaker and moderator at conferences.

About the Diplomatic Council

This book is published by the Diplomatic Council (DC): DC Publishing. The Diplomatic Council combines a global thinktank, a worldwide business network and a charity foundation in a unique organisation with consultative status at the United Nations.

DC members, like the author of this book, are firmly convinced that economic diplomacy is a solid foundation for international understanding and peaceful relations between nations. Based on this understanding, the Diplomatic Council translates the goal of global international understanding into an economic mandate. The methodology of a global economic network is combined with the diplomatic level of communication between the nations of the world. With this in mind, the Diplomatic Council is made up of personalities from the fields of diplomacy, business and society who have been selected with a sense of proportion and who are widely accepted, highly competent and whose values are in line with the basic pillars of the Diplomatic Council. We also welcome companies for whom corporate social responsibility is more than just a buzzword.

Further Information: www.diplomatic-council.org

Books from DC Publishing

How to avoid World War III – A plea for peace, Hang Nguyen, Jamal Qaiser, 244 pages, ISBN 978-3-947818-73-0

War in Europe – How Europe lost its independence and became a battlefield, Andreas Dripke, Hang Nguyen, Jamal A. Qaiser, Dr. Horst Walther, 236 pages, paperback, ISBN 978-3-98674-030-6

When China and Russia join forces... – The challenge for the free world, Andreas Dripke, Hang Nguyen, Jamal Qaiser, 236 pages, paperback, ISBN 978-3-98674-022-1

My nuclear button is bigger — America vs. North Korea. Jamal Qaiser, 184 pages, paperback, ISBN 978-3-947818-01-3

Simmering Kashmir, Jamal Qaiser, Sadaf Taimur, 110 pages, paperback, ISBN 978-3-947818-11-2

The Western Fiasco: Failure in Afghanistan, Syria, and Ukraine, Hang Nguyen, Jamal Qaiser, 144 pages, paperback, ISBN 978-3-98674-001-6

Afghanistan – The Battered Land, Jamal Qaiser, Sadaf Taimur, 112 pages, paperback, ISBN 978-3-98674-003-0

The Battle for Taiwan – The most dangerous island of the World, Jamal Qaiser, Dr. Horst Walther, 236 pages, paperback, ISBN 978-3-98674-050-4

The Nuclear Thread – The risks of nuclear power are enormous, Jamal Qaiser, Marc Ruberg, 252 pages, paperback, ISBN 978-3-98674-048-1

The Battle for Water – The Challenge of the 21st Century, Claude Piel, 336 pages, paperback, ISBN 978-3-98674-071-9

Prosperity and Economic Growth without Regrets – Climate Rescure YES – Deindustrialization NO, Jean Pütz, Andreas Dripke, 136 pages, paperback, ISBN 978-3-98674-104-4

Europe and the Emerging New Global Order, Dr. Alina Bârgăoanu, Răzvan Ceuca, Simona Cojocaru, Stacy A. Cummings, Dr. Judith Curry, Andreas Dripke, Dorin Gal, Dr. Christoph Heusgen, Stephan J. Kramer, Prof. Dr. Heinrich Kreft, Ciro Mandolini, Michael Mattis, Hang Nguyen, Jamal Qaiser, Jochen M. Richter, Marc Ruberg, Prof. Dr. Peter Schallenberg, Dr. Harald Schönfeld, André Schulte-Südhoff, George Scutaru, Dr. Horst Walther, hardcover, ISBN 978-3-98674-123-5

Bibliography

Benes, Jaromir; Michael Kumhof (2012): "The Chicago Plan Revisited", IMF Working Paper WP/12/202

Dittmar, Helga; Bond, Rod; Hurst, Megan; Kasser, Tim (2014): "The relationship between materialism and personal well-being: a meta-analysis", University of Sussex, Journal of Personality and Social Psychology Volume 107, S. 879-924

FAO, IFAD, UNICEF, WFP and WHO (2022): "The State of Food Security and Nutrition in the World 2022: Repurposing food and agricultural policies to make healthy diets more affordable", FAO, Rome

Repurposing food and agricultural policies to make healthy diets more affordable. Rome, FAO

Guterres, António (2021): „Climate action for people and planet: the time is now", Malaysia, https://www.un.org/sg/en/content/sg/articles/2021-04-18/climate-action-for-people-and-planet-the-time-now

Indset, Anders (2019): Quantenwirtschaft – Was kommt nach der Digitalisierung?, E-Book, deutsche Ausgabe, Econ, Ullstein Buchverlage, Berlin

International Monetary Fund (2021): „World Economic Outlook: Recovery during a Pandemic – Health Concerns, Supply Disruptions, Price Pressures", Washington DC

IPCC (2021), Climate Change 2021: The Physical Science Basis, Working Group I contribution to the Sixth Assessment Report of the Intergovernmental Panel on Climate Change, University Press, Cambridge

Jackson, Tim (2017): Wohlstand ohne Wachstum – Grundlagen für eine zukunftsfähige Wirtschaft – Das Update, oekom verlag, München

Kasser Tim (2003), The High Price of Materialism, Bradford Books, Cambridge/Massachusetts, The MIT Press

Lange, Steffen; Tilman Santarius et al. (2022): „ Digital Reset. Redirecting Technologies for the Deep Sustainability Transformation", TU Berlin, Berlin

Meadows, Dennis; Donella Meadows; Erich Zahn; Peter Milling (1972): Die Grenzen des Wachstums – Bericht des Club of Rome zur Lage der Menschheit, Deutsche Verlags-Anstalt, Stuttgart

Posse, Dirk (2015): „Zukunftsfähige Unternehmen in einer Postwachstumsgesellschaft. Eine theoretische und empirische Untersuchung", Schriften der Vereinigung für Ökologische Ökonomie, Heidelberg

Reischmann, Markus (2014): "Staatsverschuldung in Extrahaushalten: Historischer Überblick und Implikationen für die Schuldenbremse in Deutschland", Ifo Working Paper No. 175

Seligman, Edwin Robert Anderson (1927): Installment Selling, Harper & Brothers, New York, London

Sinn, Hans-Werner (2021): Die wundersame Geldvermehrung – Staatsverschuldung, Negativzinsen, Inflation, Herder, Freiburg im Breisgau

UNEP (2016): „ Global Material Flows and Resource Productivity – An Assessment Study of the UNEP International Resource Panel", United Nations Environment Programme (UNEP), Paris

Wildner, Tobias Maximilian; Johannes Förster; Bernd Hansjürgens (2022): " Sustainable Finance – Die Berücksichtigung von Biodiversität und Ökosystemleistungen: Bestandsaufnahme, vorläufige Bewertung und Handlungsempfehlungen", Helmholtz-Zentrum für Umweltforschung – UFZ, Leibzig

Zeh, Juli (2022): Über Menschen, btb Verlag, München

References and Notes

[1] Donella and Dennis L. Meadows: Limits to Growth (1972, original title The Limits to Growth), study on the systemic behaviour of the earth as an economic space up to the year 2100

[2] Antonio Guterres, „Climate action for people and planet: the time is now", 18. April 2021, Malaysia

[3] https://www.boerse-muenchen.de/suedseiten/846/Grenzenloses-Wachstum-in-einer-begrenzten-Welt

[4] Tim Jackson "Prosperity without growth - the update", p. 325; Defra study 2007

[5] Tim Jackson "Prosperity without growth - the update", p. 105; Defra study 2007

[6] https://clubofrome.de/historie/

[7] https://en.wikipedia.org/wiki/Tim_Kasser

[8] https://www.gluecksdetektiv.de/the-high-price-of-materialism-von-tim-kasser/

[9] https://www.cusp.ac.uk/about/fellowship/h_dittmar/

[10] https://www.bundesfinanzministerium.de/Content/DE/Interviews/2021/2021-06-19-t-online.html

[11] https://www.bundesregierung.de/breg-de/themen/nachhaltigkeitspolitik/nachhaltigkeitsstrategie-1124112

[12] Deutsche Nachhaltigkeitsstrategie – Weiterentwicklung 2021 – Kurzfassung

[13] https://blog.zeit.de/herdentrieb/2019/07/18/wachstum-vs-umwelt-ein-unloesbarer-konflikt_11386

[14] Greenpeace-Recherche, 28.05.2021; Frontal21; Panorama, 20. Mai 2021

[15] Butterberge und Bauernsorgen, Jantje Hannover | 14.06.2017, Deutschlandfunk

[16] FAO. 2021. World Food and Agriculture - Statistical Yearbook 2021. Rome. https://doi.org/10.4060/cb4477en

[17] „Dünger für den Klimawandel", Medienmitteilung der Forschungs-anstalt Art am 4.2.2010 und taz.de/Umweltbelastung-durch-Duenger/!5635932/ vom 19.11.2019

[18] Nitratbericht 2020 der Bundesrepublik Deutschland – bmuv.de/fileadmin/Daten_BMU/Download_PDF/Binnengewaesser/nitratbericht_2020_bf.pdf

[19] greenpeace.de/engagieren/nachhaltiger-leben/erdueberlastungstag-routinen-durchbrechen; footprintnet-work.org

[20] Food and Agriculture Organization of the United Nations (FAO) 2019

[21] United Nations Environment Programme (UNEP) 2021

[22] The State of Food Security and Nutrition in the World 2022, FAO 2022

[23] https:\\frontex.europa.eu

[24] https://www.tagesschau.de vom 11.01.2022

[25] https://www.unhcr.org/globaltrends

[26] heute Xpress ZDF vom 10.11.2023; https://www.spiegel.de/wissenschaft/tuvalu-australien-bietet-allen-einwohnern-der-insel-aufnahme-als-klimafluechtlinge-a-c53fa233-173b-4afb-aa84-d77c76e5f0bc

[27] https://www.dw.com/de/erbitterter-streit-um-migration-pr%C3%A4gt-eu-gipfel/a-66084819

[28] Communication from the commission to the european parliament, the council, the european economic and social committee and the committee of the regions on the report on migration and asylum – corrigendum, brussels, 12.1.2023 c(2023) 219 final

[29] Mitteilung der Kommission - Ein neues Migrations- und Asylpaket, Brüssel, den 23.9.2020; https://eur-lex.europa.eu/legal-content/DE/TXT/?uri=CELEX%3A52020DC0609

[30] https://www.europarl.europa.eu/news/de/headlines/society/20170629STO78630/asyl-und-migration-zahlen-und-fakten; https://www.europarl.europa.eu/news/de/headlines/priorities/migration/20170627STO78418/die-reform-des-gemeinsamen-europaischen-asylsystems

[31] https://www.weltderwunder.de/die-geschichte-des-privatkredits-so-fing-mit-krediten-alles-an/

[32] Edwin Robert Anderson Seligman, Installment selling, 1927, Vol. I., S. 14

[33] https://de.statista.com/statistik/daten/studie/6804/umfrage/kredite-an-privatpersonen-in-deutschland/

[34] https://de.statista.com/statistik/daten/studie/159289/umfrage/konsumausgaben-privater-haushalte-in-deutschland-zeitreihe/

[35] Statistisches Bundesamt(Destatis) 2023; Genesis Datenbank

[36] https://www.t-online.de/nachrichten/deutschland/innenpolitik/id_100281640/bundesverfassungsgericht-kippt-nachtragshaushalt-60-milliarden-haushaltsloch.html

References and Notes

[37] Bundesrechnungshof Bericht vom 25. August 2023

[38] Bundesrechnungshof Bericht vom 25.August 2023

[39] Bundesrechnungshof Bericht vom 25. August 2023

[40] Markus Reischmann, „Staatsverschuldung in Extrahaushalten: Historischer Überblick und Implikationen für die Schuldenbremse Deutschland", ifo Institut - Leibnitz-Institut für Wirtschafsforschung, Universität München, Ifo Working Paper No. 175

[41] Reischmann, ebenda

[42] https://www.bundeshaushalt.de/DE/Bundeshaushalt-digital/bundeshaushalt-digital.html

[43] https://www.deutsche-finanzagentur.de/fms/finanzmarktstabilisierungsfonds/fms-auf-einen-blick

[44] World Economic Outlook Database des IMF, April 2023; www.imf.org

[45] https://www.zeit.de/wirtschaft/2023-01/staatshilfen-unternehmen-deutschland-eu-vorn

[46] https://www.accounting-for-transparency.de/de/news/gbp-monitor-mehr-als-die-haelfte-der-unternehmen-erhielt-corona-hilfen-krisenunternehmen-fordern-jetzt-weitere-staatshilfen/#

[47] US-Schuldenbremse: Droht ein Staatsbankrott der USA? | tagesschau.de, 17.05.2023

[48] Congressional Budget Office (CBO), An Update to the Budget Outlook: 2023 to 2033 (May 12, 2023), www.cbo.gov/publications/59096

[49] CBO, ebenda S. 5

[50] https://www.fuw.ch/article/chronologie-der-finanzkrise

[51] Hans-Werner Sinn, „Die wundersame Geldvermehrung", Herder 2021, S. 65

[52] Hans-Werner Sinn, ebenda, S. 68

[53] Hans-Werner Sinn, ebenda, S. 90

[54] https://theconversation.com/ecb-unleashes-the-trillion-euro-bazooka-but-how-will-it-work-36536

[55] https://www.ecb.europa.eu/press/key/date/2018/html/ecb.sp180129.en.html

[56] https://www.europarl.europa.eu/summits/lis1_de.htm#I

[57] Karliczek: Innovationen für eine klimaneutrale Zukunft erforschen und Ambitionen für ... | Presseportal Bundesministerium für Bildung und Forschung, 02.11.2021

[58] https://openai.com

[59] Digitalization for Sustainability (D4S), 2022: Digital Reset. Redirecting Technologies for the Deep Sustainability Transformation. Berlin: TU Berlin. http://dx.doi.org/10.14279/depositonce-16187

[60] https://www.fr.de/wirtschaft/ki-studie-strom-verbrauch-umwelt-klimawandel-energie-zr-92745772.html; siehe auch: https://www.sciencedirect.com/science/article/abs/pii/S2542435123003653

[61] https://publications.jrc.ec.europa.eu/repository/handle/JRC135926

[62] https://www.bundestag.de/presse/hib/kurzmeldungen-914208, Energieverbrauch der IKT-Infrastrukturen in Deutschland, 6. Oktober 2022

[63] https://www.bitkom.org/Bitkom/Publikationen/Studie-Rechenzentren-in-Deutschland, Update 2023

[64] https://arxiv.org/abs/2304.03271, Update vom 29. Oktober 2023

[65] https://www.t-online.de/finanzen/die-anleger/id_100319610/boerse-2024-nvidia-microsoft-google-geht-die-rallye-mit-ki-weiter-.html

[66] https://www.blog2social.com/de/blog/social-media-nutzer/

[67] https://www.resourcepanel.org/global-material-flows-database

[68] Posse, Dirk (2015): Zukunftsfähige Unternehmen in einer Postwachstumsgesellschaft. Eine theoretische und empirische Untersuchung, Schriften der Vereinigung für Ökologische Ökonomie, ISBN 978-3-9811006-2-4, Vereinigung für Ökologische Ökonomie, Heidelberg, http://nbn-resolving.de/urn:nbn:de:101:1-201704231355 , http://www.voeoe.de/publikationen

[69] Digitalization for Sustainability (D4S), 2022: Digital Reset, S. 23

[70] https://data.worldbank.org; World Bank staff estimates based on sources and methods in World Bank's "The Changing Wealth of Nations: Measuring Sustainable Development in the New Millennium" (2011).

[71] https://data.worldbank.org; PM2.5 air pollution, population exposed to levels exceeding WHO guideline value (% of total); Vergleichswerte 2017

[72] Anders Indset, „Quantenwirtschaft – Was kommt nach der Digitalisierung?", 4. Vollständig aktualisierte und erweiterte Auflage, Econ, 2020

[73] International Monetary Fund. 2021. World Economic Outlook: Recovery during a Pandemic—Health Concerns, Supply Disruptions, Price Pressures. Washington, DC, October, Box 1.2

[74] https://www.nationalgeographic.de/wissenschaft/2023/03/gluecksforschung-was-wir-wirklich-brauchen-um-gluecklich-zu-sein-psychologie-skandinavien-deutschland

[75] siehe Ziff. 67 ebenda

References and Notes

[76] https://publishing.blog/von-der-ueberzeugung-und-dem-nachhaltigen-erfolg/

[77] Gesetz über die unternehmerischen Sorgfaltspflichten zur Vermeidung von Menschenrechtsverletzungen in Lieferketten (Lieferkettensorgfaltspflichtengesetz - LkSG)

[78] https://www.tagesschau.de/investigativ/rbb/lieferkettengesetz-111.html

[79] https://www.bpb.de/kurz-knapp/hintergrund-aktuell/268127/vor-fuenf-jahren-textilfabrik-rana-plaza-in-bangladesch-eingestuerzt/

[80] https://www.spiegel.de/ausland/kobaltfoerderung-im-kongo-der-alb-traumstoff-a-bcee9c56-86e5-46b2-8f82-85ccb1104160

[81] A global village in India, Johanna Treblin/sp, 2. Mai 2013

[82] www.deutsches-schulportal.de; Florentine Anders, 26. August 2022, aktualisiert am 22. August 2023

[83] Tim Jackson, ebenda S. 208

[84] https://de.statista.com/themen/11806/uebergewicht-und-fettleibigkeit/

[85] IDF Diabetes Atlas 2021 – 10th edition; www.diabetesatlas.org

[86] https://www.bundesnetzagentur.de/SharedDocs/Pressemitteilungen/DE/2023/20230106_RueckblickGasversorgung.html

[87] Bundesnetzagentur, Rückblick: Gasversorgung im Jahr 2023

[88] WirtschaftsWoche, Wie groß wird das Uiguren-Problem der Autokonzerne noch?, 22. Februar 2024

[89] WirtschaftsWoche, Volkswagen hat die Wahl: E-Autos oder Menschenrechte, 29. Februar 2024

[90] WiWo, ebenda

[91] 6. Sachstandsbericht des IPCC, Arbeitsgruppe I, SPM-33

[92] Posse, Dirk (2015), S. 73

[93] https://www.patagonia.com/company-history/

[94] Indset, Anders (2019), „Quantenwirtschaft: Was kommt nach der Digitalisierung?", Pos. 410, Ullstein eBooks, Kindle-Version

[95] https://de.statista.com/statistik/daten/studie/1126144/umfrage/woechentliche-arbeitszeit-in-deutschland/

[96] https://de.wikipedia.org/wiki/Bruttonationalglück

[97] Wikipedia, ebenda

[98] https://happiness-report.s3.amazonaws.com/2023/WHR+23.pdf

[99] https://de.wikipedia.org/wiki/Enquete-Kommission_Wachstum,_Wohlstand,_Lebensqualität

[100] https://www.bundestag.de/webarchiv/textarchiv /2010/32467716_kw48_ de_ wohlstandsenquete-203414

[101] Schlussbericht der Enquete-Kommission „Wachstum, Wohlstand, Lebensqualität – Wege zu nachhaltigem Wirtschaften und gesellschaftlichem Fortschritt in der Sozialen Marktwirtschaft", Deutscher Bundestag Drucksache 17/13300, 03.05.2013

[102] Vgl. hierzu auch: https://www.imzuwi.org/index.php/79-ueber-uns/176-w-indikatoren

[103] https://www.handelsblatt.com/politik/konjunktur/jahreswirtschaftsbericht-kein-akademisches-trockenschwimmen-wie-habeck-wohlstand-neu-definiert/28011264.html

[104] https://www.umweltbundesamt.de/publikationen/wohlfahrtsmessung-in-deutschland

[105] https://www.imk-boeckler.de/fpdf/HBS-008250/p_imk_study_78_2022.pdf

[106] https://www.umweltbundesamt.de/print/47344

[107] IMK-Study Nr. 78 STUDY, Februar 2022, Hans-Böckler-Stiftung, S. 28 ff.

[108] ZDF-Sendung MAITHINK X – Die Show, E-Fuel vs E-Auto: Mythos Technologieoffenheit vom 24.03.2024

[109] www.reparaturbonus.at

[110] https://germany.representation.ec.europa.eu/news/recht-auf-reparatur-eu-kommission-begrusst-einigung-auf-neue-verbraucherrechte-2024-02-02_de

[111] https://www.ioew.de/news/article/reparieren-erleichtern-wie-die-politik-langlebige-produkte-foerdern-kann

[112] siehe https://www.ifeu.de/fileadmin/uploads/Praxis-Handbuch.pdf

[113] https://www.ibg.at/menschenleere_fabrik/; Studie Frauenhofer-Institut „Produktionsarbeit der Zukunft – Industrie 4.0"

[114] Mirjam Moll, Neue Zürcher Zeitung vom 25.01.2024, Bertelsmann-Studie berechnet massiven Lehrerüberschuss in Grundschulen bis 2035

[115] Tim Jackson, ebenda, S. 247ff.

[116] BaFin - Fachartikel - Nachhaltigkeit: Daran kommt niemand mehr vorbei

[117] BaFin – Fachartikel, ebenda

References and Notes

[118] Wildner, T.M., Förster, J., Hansjürgens, B. (2022) Sustainable Finance – Die Berücksichtigung von Biodiversität und Ökosystemleistungen: Bestandsaufnahme, vorläufige Bewertung und Handlungsempfehlungen. Studie im Auftrag des NABU.

[119] https://finance.ec.europa.eu/capital-markets-union-and-financial-markets/company-reporting-and-auditing/company-reporting/corporate-sustainability-reporting_en

[120] https://www.financeforbiodiversity.org/about-the-pledge/

[121] https://www.imf.org/external/pubs/ft/wp/2012/wp12202.pdf

[122] Michael Kumhof, „Financial reform for a sustainable economy": https://youtu.be/YnAtHbDptj8

[123] Bundesbank Monatsberichte, 69. Jg, Nr. 4, April 2017, S. 33-36

[124] Wikipedia: Letzte Generation

[125] U.a. Ziff. 27 United Nations A/RES/70/1, 21 October 2015, Resolution adopted by the General Assembly on 25 September 2015

[126] https://www.bundesregierung.de/breg-de/themen/nachhaltigkeitspolitik/nachhaltig-wirtschaften-276606, 16. August 2023

[127] Schlussbericht der Enquete-Kommission „Wachstum, Wohlstand, Lebensqualität", Vorwort der Vorsitzenden

[128] siehe Ziff. 28 United Nations A/RES/70/1, 21 October 2015, Resolution adopted by the General Assembly on 25 September 2015

[129] https://www.bundesregierung.de/breg-de/themen/nachhaltigkeitspolitik/nachhaltig-wirtschaften-276606

[130] Juli Zeh, „Über Menschen", btb-Verlag 2022

[131] IPCC AR6 WGI Full Report, SPM-17, Seite 47

[132] IPCC, 2021: Summary for Policymakers. In: Climate Change 2021: The Physical Science Basis. Contribution of Working Group I to the Sixth Assessment Report of the Intergovernmental Panel on Climate Change [Masson-Delmotte, V., P. Zhai, A. Pirani, S. L. Connors, C. Péan, S. Berger, N. Caud, Y. Chen, L. Goldfarb, M. I. Gomis, M. Huang, K. Leitzell, E. Lonnoy, J.B.R. Matthews, T. K. Maycock, T. Waterfield, O. Yelekçi, R. Yu and B. Zhou (eds.)]. Cambridge University Press. In Press, S. 19

[133] https://www.lpb-bw.de/ipcc: Weltklimabericht 2023 aktuell - Klimabericht IPCC - IPCC-Berichte: Sachstandsberichte zur Klimaforschung - Zusammenfassung (lpb-bw.de)

www.ingramcontent.com/pod-product-compliance
Ingram Content Group UK Ltd.
Pitfield, Milton Keynes, MK11 3LW, UK
UKHW032216171224
452513UK00010B/505